Women's Rights

Edited by Jennifer Curry

Editorial Advisor Lynn M. Messina

The Reference Shelf
Volume 77 • Number 4

The H. W. Wilson Company
2005

The Reference Shelf

The books in this series contain reprints of articles, excerpts from books, addresses on current issues, and studies of social trends in the United States and other countries. There are six separately bound numbers in each volume, all of which are usually published in the same calendar year. Numbers one through five are each devoted to a single subject, providing background information and discussion from various points of view and concluding with a subject index and comprehensive bibliography that lists books, pamphlets, and abstracts of additional articles on the subject. The final number of each volume is a collection of recent speeches, and it contains a cumulative speaker index. Books in the series may be purchased individually or on subscription.

Library of Congress has cataloged this title as follows:

Women's rights / edited by Jennifer Curry; editorial advisor, Lynn M. Messina.
    p. cm. — (The reference shelf; v. 77, no. 4)
  Includes bibliographical references and index.
  ISBN 0-8242-1049-2 (alk. paper)
    1. Women's rights. 2. Women—Social conditions. 3. Women and religion. I. Curry, Jennifer. II. Messina, Lynn. III. Series.

HQ1236.W65253 2005
323.3'4—dc22

2005014527

Cover: A rally celebrating International Women's Day in Katmandu, Nepal, on March 8, 2004. (AP Photo/Binod Joshi)

Visit H.W. Wilson's Web site: www.hwwilson.com

Printed in the United States of America

The Reference Shelf®

Contents

Preface

There are approximately 3.2 billion women in the world, and given the diversity of their life experiences it is difficult to make generalizations about womankind as a whole—except to say that everywhere they are treated, to a greater or lesser extent, as the subordinates of men. While women comprise half of the world's population and are responsible for two-thirds of the world's work, they earn only about one-tenth of the world's income and own approximately one-hundredth of the world's property, according to the United Nations. Over the last century, however, women's rights activists have made tremendous strides, and an increasing number of women and men around the world are beginning to recognize that, as 2003 Nobel Peace Prize recipient Shirin Ebadi so eloquently put it, to "disregard women and bar them from active participation in political, social, economic, and cultural life would in fact be tantamount to depriving the entire population of every society of half its capability."

The modern women's rights movement was born of the Western Enlightenment but did not effect significant social change until the 20th century. Women in Europe and the United States successfully lobbied for many of the same rights as men, and their victories breathed life into the struggle for equality around the world. The movement, however, has always been met with resistance. Given the long history of Western intervention in the developing world—self-serving imperialists have often claimed to be acting in the best interest of local inhabitants—it should come as little surprise that efforts to change the traditional role of women are often met with hostility, even among some women. In recent years, women in the developing world have become increasingly outspoken in their demand for equal rights. "The idea of cultural relativism is nothing but an excuse to violate human rights," Ebadi argued in a 2005 interview. "Human rights is a universal standard. It is a component of every religion and every civilization."

Even in Western nations, some of the hard-fought gains of the past century—particularly a woman's right to control her sexuality and reproductive freedom—face increasing peril. Opponents of the feminist movement argue that activists have gone too far, claiming that programs such as affirmative action in the workplace have tipped the scales in favor of women. Yet a recent survey of starting salaries among college graduates in the United States indicates that women earn far less on average than comparably educated men.

This book addresses some of the contemporary issues that are of pivotal importance to the struggle for women's rights. The first chapter assesses the advances that women have made in the public sphere and the inequities they still face. Women may have earned the right to vote in most countries, but nowhere are they equally represented in governing bodies. Likewise, they may have earned the right to work outside of the home, but everywhere they remain the poorest of the poor. As the second chapter explains, this inequality in political and economic power translates into unequal access to health care. Women suffer from poorer health and higher mortality rates than men not only because they receive less attention from the medical profession, but also because they remain the victims of misogynistic cultural traditions. The third chapter examines another kind of pandemic affecting women's health throughout the world: violence against women. Women suffer gender-specific violence during times of war, within the domestic sphere, and as a part of traditional community practices. As economic disparity in the world increases, more women are subjected to the systematic torture and sexual violence of the global sex trade, which is discussed in detail in the fourth chapter.

The last two chapters in this book examine the greatest threat to the continued advancement of women's rights—religious fundamentalism. The fifth chapter discusses the status of Muslim women in the context of the conflict between the Western and Islamic worlds, addressing complex and politically contentious questions. Why is it that women's rights lag so far behind in the Islamic world? How do Muslim women envision their own liberation? Lest we fall prey to the ethnocentric assumption that religious fundamentalism poses a threat to only Muslim women, the sixth and final chapter examines how Christian fundamentalists are trying to roll back reproductive rights in the United States and, through international aid, in the developing world.

I would like to extend my thanks to all the authors and publications that granted their permission to use their work for this compendium. I would especially like to thank Lynn M. Messina, Sandra Watson, Paul McCaffrey, Rich Stein, and Clifford Thompson at H.W. Wilson for their role in the book's production. In addition, I would like to thank John Packer, Terence Fitzgerald, Angela Dykshorn, Sally Puleo, Dr. Gwynne L. Jenkins, Dr. Jane Gibson, and Nuchine Nobari for their helpful advice during the research for this project.

Jennifer Curry
August 2005

I. Women in the Public Sphere

Editor's Introduction

The emergence of women into what is known as the public sphere—the space outside of the home in which one interacts with society—is undoubtedly the greatest accomplishment of the previous century in women's rights. Working alongside men in business and government, women have proven themselves capable of contributing to society outside of their traditional roles as wife and mother. Inequities persist, however, and while women have won voting rights in all but a handful of countries, they lack equal representation in government in even the most liberal nations. Women everywhere still earn less than men for both professional and unskilled labor; they are the victims of outright discrimination and are discouraged from pursuing careers in higher-paying fields. Women also fill an increasing percentage of available part-time jobs. While these positions allow women the flexibility they need to also shoulder unpaid labor in the home—such as raising children and caring for elderly relatives—they confer fewer benefits and pay lower wages.

In this chapter's first article, "One Battle After Another," Sophie Bessis examines a century of advances in the struggle for women's rights—winning access to education, the right to vote, and reproductive rights—and emphasizes the work that remains. She argues that though feminism first emerged in Western societies, it has energized the movement for women's rights worldwide. Many women in the developing world reject some of the values of Western feminists, however, and are pursuing gender equity on their own terms.

As Jessica Neuwirth points out in "Unequal: A Global Perspective on Women Under the Law," sex discrimination is often legitimized by governments, written into the laws of both developing and industrialized nations around the world. Many women do not have the legal right to vote, file for divorce, refuse marital intercourse, or inherit property. There has been some progress since the Beijing Platform for Action—an agenda established by United Nations member states in 1995 to promote equality for women—but Neuwirth describes the change of pace as "lethargic."

In 1979 the United Nations adopted the Convention on the Elimination of All Forms of Discrimination Against Women (CEDAW), which requires signatories to repeal discriminatory laws and to create provisions that guard against discrimination. In "International Holdout," Ellen Chesler chastises the United States government for failing after 25 years to sign the convention, placing the country in the company of such notorious human rights offenders as Iran, Somalia, and Sudan.

In "Another Pose of Rectitude," George F. Will questions the effectiveness of CEDAW, arguing that it is open to a wide variety of interpretations and lacks means of enforcement. He argues that signing off on CEDAW gives elites the opportunity to adopt an air of moral superiority while doing little to advance women's rights.

In the following article, "Nordic Women Suffer Gender Gap Least," Jane Wardell reports that the World Economic Forum singled out the United States for criticism in May 2005 when it released its "Gender Gap Index," which ranks the status of women in 58 countries based on wage parity, representation in politics, and access to education, the labor market, and reproductive health care. Lagging behind other Western nations, the United States ranked 17th, while the Nordic countries—Sweden, Norway, Iceland, Denmark, and Finland—scored the highest overall. These countries are characterized by strong liberal societies, government transparency, generous welfare systems, and ready access for women to educational, political, and employment opportunities.

In "More Women Are Entering the Global Labour Force Than Ever Before, But Job Equality and Poverty Reduction Remain Elusive," an uncredited writer for the International Labour Organization explains that, despite explosive growth in the female workforce worldwide, women still have not attained socio-economic empowerment. Women face higher rates of unemployment than men, are compensated with lower wages, and comprise 60 percent of the 550 million of the working poor.

Aaron Bernstein examines the persistent wage gap between men and women in "Women's Pay: Why the Gap Remains a Chasm." Only about 10 percentage points of the wage gap can be attributed to outright discrimination, so the problem mostly lies with, as Bernstein says, "the conflicting needs and norms of society and employers." Women who are not saddled with traditional responsibilities in the home earn salaries nearly equivalent to their male coworkers, while women who require flexibility in their work schedule in order to rear children or care for other family members often find employers unaccommodating.

In "Employed, Yes—But Precariously," an excerpt from the Oxfam report *Trading Away Our Rights*, the authors provide evidence that globalization has unduly burdened poor women, particularly in the developing world. Many countries have rolled back labor laws to attract manufacturers, leaving workers with unhealthy working conditions and no support in their attempts to unionize.

One Battle After Another

By Sophie Bessis
UNESCO Courier, June 2000

We often hear that this will be the century of women, in light of the tremendous strides that have been made in the past 30 years or so. Although it is far too soon to confirm this prediction, it can safely be asserted that the 20th century was marked by their struggle to leave the home, where they were confined by the ancestral division of roles along gender lines. Around the world, women have campaigned to win the rights they have been denied and to build, side-by-side with men, the future of the planet.

True, such struggles had already been waged in the past, although they were deliberately shunned in official historical accounts. But the brief revolts of this special "minority," which accounts for over half of humanity, did not change the place of women in their societies. They may have ruled the roost, sometimes enjoying undeniable respect, but nevertheless they were still born to serve men and bring their husbands' descendants into the world.

Education: Their First Struggle

Yet, at the start of the 20th century, the traditional distribution of roles, seemingly legitimised by every religion and frozen in a "natural" order, began to crumble under the two-pronged assault of modernisation and women's struggle for their collective emancipation. They waged many battles to gradually obtain, despite setbacks, a change in their status—which is still far from achieved.

The first struggle of the 20th century was for education. In 1861, a young woman graduated in France with a baccalaureate, a high-school leaving exam, for the first time. In 1900, the first female university was founded in Japan. The same year, girls won the right to secondary education in Egypt and the first girls' school opened in Tunisia. Young women who could made the most of these new educational opportunities, not only to become better household managers and good educators for their children, as the main discourse of the period suggests, but also to do something unprecedented: to enter the forbidden spheres of public life, to exercise citizenship, and to participate in politics.

Throughout the 20th century, women waged a battle on two fronts: by fighting for their own rights and taking part in the major social and political emancipation movements. In 1917, the Russian Bolshevik Alexandra Kollontaï became the world's first woman cabinet minister. African American Rosa Parks triggered the civil rights movement by refusing to give up her seat to a white man on an Alabama bus in 1955. Djamila Boupacha was a heroine of Algeria's war for independence. Women were entirely committed to the goals of these movements but seldom received anything in return for participating in them. Once their countries' new masters took power, they often found themselves sent back to the kitchen. But they continued fighting for their own rights, and it is on this front that they achieved their greatest victories.

The earliest feminist movements, which first appeared in the West in the late 19th century, focused on workplace and civil rights issues. Industry needed women's labour, which was underpaid in comparison with that of their male counterparts. "Equal pay for equal work!" demanded American and European women, who began setting up their own trade unions and organizing strikes. They made unquestionable strides, but after more than one century of struggle, most women around the world still earn less pay for equal work.

The Right to Vote

The second objective of the 20th century's pioneers was participation in public life, which hinged first and foremost on having the right to vote. The struggle was long and sometimes violent, as shown by the British "suffragettes" who demonstrated in the streets or Chinese women who made their demands heard by invading their country's new parliament in 1912. Everywhere, the fierce resistance of the political world progressively yielded to determined women's movements.

Scandinavia is where women first won the right to vote and to run for election, with Finland leading the way in 1906. The First World War thrust them into the forefront, with most European women winning the right to vote in 1918 and 1919, although French and Italian women had to wait until after the Second World War to at last be recognized as citizens. Outside the West, women also organized to demand their rights. Groups were founded in Turkey, Egypt, and India. In 1930, the first congress of women from the Near and Middle East gathered in Damascus to demand equality. Throughout this period, women everywhere declared that, outside of motherhood, they had the right to be just like men, and that men could not deny them this right.

Control Over Their Own Bodies

For a while, women's rights movements took a back seat to the Second World War and liberation struggles in the European colonies. The fight against fascism and, after 1945, colonialism, mobilized all their energy. Women distinguished themselves in these struggles, but that did not suffice to establish their rights as a gender. However, the world continued to change. With independence, many women in the South won access to schooling, salaried employment, and, in a few exceptional cases, the closed world of politics. In Western countries, the post-war period saw them enter the work force on a massive scale. The gap between social reality and the discriminatory laws defended by exclusively male power structures grew wider.

In the West, the second generation of feminists emerged in the wake of the libertarian movements of 1968. Picking up where their elders left off, they broadened the scope of their demands, for late-20th-century feminists no longer aspired to the right to be "just like men." Challenging the claim of the "white male" to represent universality, their goal was to achieve equality while remaining distinct as women. The women's liberation movement that first

---

Everywhere, the fierce resistance of the political world progressively yielded to determined women's movements.

---

emerged in the American middle-class claimed the right to control one's own body. Feminists fought for contraception and abortion rights in many countries where one or both were against the law, and for autonomy and equality within the couple. "The personal is political," proclaimed women inspired by Marxism and psychoanalysis. "Workers of the world, who washes your socks?" chanted demonstrators in the streets of Paris in the 1970s. In France, the Veil law legalizing abortion unleashed emotional debate in 1974.

Many Third World women could not identify with the struggles being waged in the West and insisted on leading their own battles at their own pace. However, these Western feminist movements breathed new life into the cause. Recognizing the changes and proclaiming their intention to accelerate them, the United Nations declared 1975 "International Women's Year" and organized the first international women's conference in Mexico City.

Already proclaimed in the Universal Declaration of Human Rights in 1948, sexual equality was reasserted in 1979 by the Convention on the Abolition of All Forms of Discrimination Against Women, which became a precious emancipation tool in the North as well as the South. At U.N. conferences in Copenhagen in 1980, Nairobi in 1985, and Beijing in 1995, women from both hemispheres found common ground, demanding the right to "have a child if I want it, when I want it," rejecting Malthusian principles and claiming their place in political bodies that until then had decided the world's future without them, struggling against religious fundamentalism that jeopardizes their modest gains.

Misogyny of the Political Class

Of course, the struggle of Kuwaiti women against those who have denied them the right to vote or Indian women against the forced abortion of female foetuses is not the same as American women's battle against their own fundamentalists or French women's campaign against the misogyny of the political class. Women's movements take different approaches depending on the continent and do not necessarily have the same priorities, but the struggle has nonetheless become global during the past several decades. In the last 25 years, women have gradually increased their presence in public life, although it can hardly be said that the doors are wide open for them. From Africa to Asia, women's organizations have multiplied and acquired experience.

But their victories remain incomplete and the future is uncertain. From the nightmare of Afghan women to the ways in which equality is resisted in the so-called most advanced countries, the obstacles show that there is still a long way to go. Will women see the end of the struggle in this century that has just begun, the one which supposedly belongs to them?

Unequal

A Global Perspective on Women Under the Law

BY JESSICA NEUWIRTH
Ms., SUMMER 2004

Around the world, real discrimination against women persists—
much of it in blatant, tolerated, *legal* form. Why?

It makes no sense. The right to equality has been affirmed
repeatedly, in international law, national constitutions, and various treaties. Name them: the Universal Declaration of Human
Rights, the International Covenant on Civil and Political Rights,
the Convention on the Elimination of All Forms of Discrimination
against Women (CEDAW)—all provide for equality before the law
and equal protection. The Beijing Platform for Action, adopted at
the 1995 United Nations Fourth World Conference on Women,
states the need to "ensure equality and non-discrimination under
the law and in practice" and to "revoke any remaining laws that
discriminate on the basis of sex."

It sounds good. But the reality on the ground, in cities and villages, homes and schools, and even in the courts, is quite different.

Many discriminatory laws still relate to family law, limiting a
woman's right to marry, divorce, and remarry, and allowing for
such marital practices as polygamy. Mali, Sudan, and Yemen are
among countries with laws still mandating "wife obedience" in
marital relations. Sudan's 1991 Muslim Personal Law Act provides
that a husband's rights include being "taken care of and amicably
obeyed" by his wife. Yemen's 1992 Personal Status Act even enu-
merates the elements of wife obedience, including requirements
that a wife "must permit him [her husband] to have licit intercourse with her," that she "must obey his orders," and that "she
must not leave the conjugal home without his permission."

But if you think blatant legal discrimination is a problem only in
Muslim societies and/or developing countries, think again.

Many nations, including the United States, explicitly discriminate on the basis of sex in the transmission of citizenship: to children, depending on the sex of the parent, and/or through marriage,
depending on the sex of the spouse. The U.S. law—which gives
children born abroad and out of wedlock differing rights to citizenship, depending on whether their mothers or fathers are U.S. citizens—was upheld by the Supreme Court in 2001: Children of U.S.

mothers have a lifetime right to citizenship, while children of U.S. fathers (including all those GIs stationed overseas) must take legal steps, before turning 18, to claim citizenship.

In its 5-4 decision, the Court held that the law was justified on the basis of two governmental interests: "assuring a biological parent-child relationship exists" and a "determination to ensure that the child and the citizen parent have some demonstrated opportunity or potential to develop . . . a relationship that . . . consists of the real, everyday ties that provide a connection between child and citizen parent, and, in turn, the United States."

The majority opinion, authored by Justice Anthony M. Kennedy, did not address the fact that such a relationship was arbitrarily required by law for U.S. citizen fathers but not U.S. citizen mothers. In the dissent, Justice Sandra Day O'Connor noted, "Indeed, the majority's discussion may itself simply reflect the stereotype of male irresponsibility that is no more a basis for the validity of the classification than are stereotypes about the 'traditional' behavior patterns of women."

In many countries, criminal offenses . . . are explicitly sex-discriminatory.

Other "personal status" laws that discriminate on the basis of sex range from the denial of women's right to vote in Kuwait to the prohibition against women driving in Saudi Arabia.

Inheritance and property laws are also key areas where discrimination exists. Lesotho's laws provide that "no immovable property shall be registered in the name of a woman married in community of property." Chile's Civil Code mandates that "the marital partnership is to be headed by the husband, who shall administer the spouses' joint property as well as the property owned by his wife."

Until 2002, the law in Nepal was that daughters had the right to a share of family property only if they were at least 35 years old and unmarried; after years of effort, the Nepali Women's Movement succeeded in amending the law—but just in part: Now, daughters are born with the same right to family property as are sons, but the law requires women to *return* any such property upon marriage.

In many countries, criminal offenses—their definitions as well as rules governing admissible evidence—are explicitly sex-discriminatory. In Pakistan, for example, written legal documents concerning financial obligations must be attested to by two men, or by one man and two women. In rape cases there, four Muslim adult males must testify to witnessing the rape; there is no provision for testimony from female witnesses.

Marital rape is explicitly excluded from rape laws in many nations—for example, India, Malaysia, and Tonga. Ethiopia, Lebanon, Guatemala, and Uruguay exempt men from penalty for rape—

if they subsequently marry their victims. Northern Nigeria's penal code notes that assault is not an offense if inflicted "by a husband for the purpose of correcting his wife" so long as it "does not amount to the infliction of grievous hurt."

And in cases of so-called honor killings, men who murder their wives are exempt from punishment by law in Syria, Morocco, and Haiti. In Jordan, a campaign against "honor" killings did change the law—but only to make it gender neutral, exempting any spouse from punishment for an "honor" killing. Since virtually all such killings are perpetrated by men, this amendment removes the appearance of sex discrimination, not the discrimination itself.

Laws that explicitly discriminate are only the tip of the iceberg. The denial of equal opportunity in education and employment, exclusion from political representation, deprivation of sexual and reproductive rights, plus the use of social forces and physical violence to intimidate and subordinate women—all these are viola-

---

In cases of so-called honor killings, men who murder their wives are exempt from punishment by law in Syria, Morocco, and Haiti.

---

tions of the right to equality. In many countries, abortion is a criminal offense that burdens women with medical consequences, often fatal, of unsafely terminating a pregnancy. In some countries—the Philippines, for example—prostitution is a criminal offense for the prostituted female but not for the male customer.

In virtually all countries, there are laws, policies, and practices that, though not explicitly discriminatory, in practice deny women equality. This in itself is illegal. Whenever laws perpetuate women's inequality—even when their language appears gender neutral—they constitute discrimination in violation of international norms.

In June 2000, a Special Session of the U.N. General Assembly reviewed implementation of the Beijing Platform, five years after its adoption. An Outcome Document was adopted, outlining achievements, obstacles, and further actions to be taken by governments and by the U.N. to implement the Platform. Paragraph 21 cites gender discrimination as one such obstacle to implementation of the Platform, noting that discriminatory legislation persists. It notes, too, that new laws discriminating against women have been introduced (in Nigeria, for example).

The Document also provides that countries should review legislation "striving to remove discriminatory provisions as soon as possible, preferably by 2005." The preliminary draft had noted 2005 as an unequivocal target date for the elimination of discriminatory laws; the final document reflects a compromise, with the target date stated as a preference.

Elimination of such laws doesn't require financial expenditure. It requires political will, in the form of a legislative act. This political will is obviously absent; the very notion of setting a target date five years into the future—merely to remove explicitly discriminatory legal provisions—was hotly contested at the General Assembly Special Session.

Still, there has been progress. A number of countries have repealed discriminatory laws since the adoption of the 1995 Beijing Platform for Action. Venezuela adopted a new constitution that removed discriminatory citizenship provisions. Mexico rescinded a law that required a woman to wait 300 days from the dissolution of marriage before remarrying. Turkey rescinded a law that designated the husband as the head of a marital union, responsible for all family savings. Papua New Guinea removed the exemption of marital rape from its definition of rape, and Costa Rica removed the exemption from punishment for rapists who subsequently married their victims. Switzerland amended a law that had barred women in the military from using arms other than for self-defense, thus opening all military functions/responsibilities to women.

In 2001 (after threat of financial sanctions from the European Commisson), France rescinded a law prohibiting women from night employment in industrial "workplaces of any nature, be they public or private, civil, or religious, even if such establishments are for the purpose of professional education or charitable work."

Laws are changing. But the pace of change is lethargic, while the need for change is urgent. The substantial gap between the rhetoric and the reality of sex-equality rights indicates the lack of meaningful commitment to applicable treaty obligations and commitments governments have made. Public pressure can play a role in helping to overcome such lethargy.

The diplomatic community can feel shame under pressure, and that itself is a powerful technique too rarely used by governments, themselves fearful of the same spotlight. NGOs, of course, continually work to shatter the silence. But until governments match their interest in setting standards with an interest in implementing the standards they set, the integrity of the legal process will remain a question. That there are any laws explicitly discriminating against women is unacceptable, and must be universally seen and acknowledged as such—even in the diplomatic corridors of the United Nations.

International Holdout

By Ellen Chesler
The American Prospect, October 2004

Twenty-five years ago this December, the General Assembly of the United Nations adopted the Convention on the Elimination of All Forms of Discrimination Against Women (CEDAW), a global "bill of rights" that is both visionary and comprehensive. In the waning days of his presidency, Jimmy Carter hurriedly signed the convention and sent it to the U.S. Senate for ratification. But it has languished there ever since, held up by intransigent conservatives opposing both international obligations and women's rights. One hundred seventy-seven countries around the world have signed the treaty, leaving the United States among a handful of so-called rogue states—including Iran, Somalia, and Sudan—that have failed to do so.

For years the famously cantankerous Jesse Helms led the attack against CEDAW, calling it the work of "radical feminists" with an "anti-family agenda." "I do not intend to be pushed around by discourteous, demanding women," he said provocatively on the Senate floor in 1999. Helms, of course, is no longer around to exercise his veto, but George W. Bush is now standing in the way, even as he justifies two wars against fundamentalism, at least partly in the name of advancing the status of women abroad.

Around the world, empowering women is now widely considered essential to expanding economic growth, reducing poverty, improving public health, sustaining the environment, and consolidating transitions from tyranny to democracy. A near-universal consensus is calling for fundamental changes in practices that have denied rights to women for centuries. If the Democrats retake the White House and/or the Senate, it will be time to insist that the United States finally become an official party to the agreement.

CEDAW's passage in 1979 marked the beginning of formal UN commitment to advancing the status of women. It was meant to realize the original promise of the landmark 1948 Universal Declaration on Human Rights, which entitles every individual to the exercise of the rights and freedoms it sets forth—without distinction of any kind, including race, religion, ethnicity, class, or sex. In this sense, CEDAW serves as a recognition of the transformative potential of human-rights doctrine on personal relationships, not just political ones.

With the advent of the Cold War and the postcolonial rise of so many totalitarian regimes, human-rights discourse principally focused on the public realm, on protecting individuals from arbitrary state authority and brutality. CEDAW marked the beginning of a new era in using the language of human rights to challenge long-established social and cultural traditions, along with civic and political ones, that diminish women.

CEDAW acknowledges the importance of women's traditional obligations within the family, but it also establishes new norms for women's participation in all dimensions of life. It catalogs a broad range of rights in marriage and family relations, including property, inheritance, and access to health care, with an explicit mention of family planning (though not of abortion). It demands equality for women as citizens with full access to suffrage, political representation, and other legal benefits; it also declares their right to education, including professional and vocational training and the elimination of gender stereotypes and segregation. Lastly, it establishes their rights as workers deserving equal remuneration, Social Security benefits, and protection from sexual harassment and workplace discrimination on the grounds of marriage or maternity.

> *CEDAW is not "self-executing"; it requires that domestic laws be passed to implement its provisions.*

In a number of countries—including South Africa, Brazil, Australia, Zambia, Sri Lanka, Uganda, and, most recently (if ironically), Afghanistan and Iraq—treaty provisions have been incorporated into constitutions or bills of rights for women. Elsewhere, the treaty has been used to pass specific laws governing workplace practices and property rights, improving access to girls' education, extending maternity leave and child care, requiring legal protection for victims of domestic violence, outlawing female genital cutting, expanding family-planning access, and curbing sexual trafficking.

Like all international covenants, the treaty respects national sovereignty and does not impose absolute legal obligations. CEDAW is not "self-executing"; it requires that domestic laws be passed to implement its provisions. It also provides for the granting of "reservations, understandings and declarations," if necessary, to accommodate local variations from its standards. Indeed, many signatories do not live up to its obligations, an admitted weakness of many human-rights statutes. Still, ratifying countries are obliged to submit regular reports to the United Nations, where a CEDAW committee semi-annually reviews each country's progress toward implementation and reports to the General Assembly with recommendations for improvement.

Conservative opponents of the treaty in the United States regularly misrepresent and ridicule the work of this committee. Their most common canards repeat the same specious claims that earlier defeated the Equal Rights Amendment to the U.S. Constitution:

that CEDAW abridges parental rights, threatens single-sex education, mandates combat military service for women, demands legal abortion, sanctions homosexuality and same-sex marriage, prohibits the celebration of Mother's Day, and the like—all not true, of course.

Another reason it has been hard to generate energy in support of America's signing of the convention is a widespread but false assumption that American women don't really need it, protected as they are by a substantial body of U.S. case law. U.S. Supreme Court Justices Stephen Breyer and Ruth Bader Ginsburg counter this claim. Both have spoken widely of the positive benefits of applying international standards in pursuing equality under U.S. law. Their concurring opinion in *Grutter v. Bollinger*, the recent case upholding the use of affirmative action by the University of Michigan, cited the International Convention on the Elimination of all Forms of Racial Discrimination, which the United States has ratified and which obliges governments to look not only at intent but also at outcome in judging racist practices. Ginsburg, in a recent article defending workplace affirmative-action policies for women and promoting paid family leave and child care (benefits this country still does not provide), encouraged the use of CEDAW as a justification for change.

Some, like Leila Milani of the Working Group on Ratification of CEDAW, argue that the convention might also be used to encourage equal representation in Washington, where the U.S. Congress and all executive agencies are exempt from affirmative-action laws. This is particularly important because, despite substantial gains, women hold only 14 of 100 seats in the U.S. Senate, 59 of 435 in the House of Representatives, and, elsewhere around the country, approximately 20 percent of state legislative positions.

This, of course, is nowhere near the minimum goals for legislative participation by women that Afghanistan and Iraq both included in their constitutions (with U.S. encouragement). Support for CEDAW is growing nationally, though. A September 2003 Zogby poll for the Foreign Policy Association shows that when the treaty is explained, seven in 10 Americans assign high importance to it, ranking it above the Kyoto Protocol on the environment and on par with agreements on nuclear weapons. Several states have already passed resolutions urging Senate action. And in San Francisco, a young women's group called Women's Institute for Leadership Development for Human Rights (WILD) successfully pushed for the passage of a local ordinance applying CEDAW's principles to municipal laws and demanding a gender audit of city hiring and contracting. Similar efforts are under way in New York and Iowa.

For social activists looking to educate the public on women's issues, a campaign to ratify CEDAW could be an effective tool, especially in light of Bush administration backsliding on women's issues such as workplace discrimination and reproductive health. A grass-roots campaign for CEDAW has extended its reach considerably in recent years. There is a sizable organizational infrastructure already in place. Media strategies have been developed through an initiative of the Communications Consortium Media Center in Washington. Lobbying strategies are also being developed through the CEDAW Working Group and the Women's Edge Coalition, both of which report growing interest from Democrats and Republican moderates in the Senate, including Richard Lugar, the highly considered Foreign Relations Committee chairman, who replaced Helms when the North Carolina senator retired.

A logjam remains in the Bush administration, to be sure, but a resolute electorate, pushed by a public education and mobilization effort with real muscle behind it, may be able to change that.

Another Pose of Rectitude

BY GEORGE F. WILL
NEWSWEEK, SEPTEMBER 2, 2002

George Orwell's axiom about intellectuals—that some ideas are so silly that only intellectuals will embrace them—needs a corollary that covers U.S. senators: No international agreement is so grandiose in its ambitions and so unclear about the obligations it imposes that it cannot receive the support of many U.S. senators. Consider the Convention on the Elimination of All Forms of Discrimination Against Women (CEDAW).

The Senate Foreign Relations Committee has again, as in 1994, endorsed CEDAW, which the United Nations adopted in 1979. By now 170 countries have accepted its provisions, such as the obligation to "take all appropriate measures to modify the social and cultural patterns of conduct of men and women, with a view to achieving the elimination of prejudices and customary and all other practices which are based on the idea of the inferiority or the superiority of either of the sexes or on stereotyped roles for men and women."

Such unlikely exponents of advanced feminism as Iraq, Saudi Arabia, and North Korea have ratified CEDAW. Evidently provisions like the one just cited are, to say no more, construed rather differently from place to place, and are enforced nowhere.

With what "appropriate" measures would one tidy up all those "patterns," both social and cultural? Well, CEDAW's apparatus includes a committee composed of 23 "experts of high moral standing and competence" who assess signatories' progress in implementing CEDAW's provisions. Nineteen of the 23 countries from which the "experts" come have been censured by the U.S. government for abuse of women's rights.

The committee has announced itself "concerned" about "the continuing prevalence of . . . such [stereotypical] symbols as Mothers' Day and a Mothers' Award" in Belarus. The ideology that infuses CEDAW is that motherhood is a backward social convention, not a biological fact. Hence the committee also has "strongly" urged Armenia "to combat the traditional stereotype of women in 'the noble role of mother'." Regarding Slovenia, the committee is "concerned" that more than 70 percent of children under 3 are cared for by family members and other individuals and therefore might "miss out on educational and social opportunities offered in formal day care." The committee urges China to legalize prostitution. And so on.

CEDAW is mostly an exhortation to be nice, with niceness understood largely as equality before the law, and the law delivering the panoply of benefits that Europeans call social democracy, including a sacramental regard for abortion rights. Which means that this, like many other pieces of international parchment, pertains only to people living in places, such as Saudi Arabia, where it is impotent.

CEDAW is a gesture, and not a harmless one, because it encourages the bad habit of moral preening, whereby elites give themselves the pleasure of striking poses of rectitude, and confuse their pleasure with national virtue. In 1994 the Foreign Relations Committee minority opposed to CEDAW wrote: "CEDAW exemplifies a disturbing trend among executive branch officials and non-governmental organizations to focus resources and political will on the U.S. ratification of treaties rather than on promoting the norms represented by those treaties in the countries where they are under attack."

CEDAW is mostly an exhortation to be nice, with niceness understood largely as equality before the law.

Perhaps the most important emancipator of Japanese women was Gen. Douglas MacArthur, who made women's suffrage occupation policy. The liberators of Afghan women wore U.S. battle dress.

The Bush administration, kicking this can down the road, says it wants to study CEDAW. It should study this:

Recent floods had not yet crested in Dresden, Prague, and elsewhere when some Europeans were blaming this misfortune on U.S. "unilateralism." They meant that there would not have been such floods were it not for the U.S. judgment that the Kyoto accords on global warming, as written, are decidedly not in the U.S. interest. When Congress passed and President Bush signed the new law concerning corporate governance and accounting, there were European murmurings about U.S. "unilateralism." The purport of the murmurs was that because Europeans invest and otherwise do business in America, it is improper for American law pertaining to business to be shaped without formal consultation with foreigners.

It is understandable that Europeans, painfully aware of the uses to which many of their nations put sovereignty in the 20th century, are retreating from sovereignty in the 21st. They are "pooling" their sovereignties in the European Union and other multinational institutions, and shedding it by promiscuously embracing supervision, of sorts, under instruments like CEDAW.

CEDAW's advocates are dismayed that America is the only developed democratic nation that has not ratified it. But that actually testifies to how uniquely well developed America's democratic political culture is.

In 2000, 35 senators, 32 Democrats, supported CEDAW, but ratification, which has been pending on the Foreign Relations Committee calendar for 22 years, would require 67 votes, so it will still be pending in 2024. As will complaints about U.S. "unilateralism," meaning self-government.

Nordic Women Suffer Gender Gap Least

By Jane Wardell
Associated Press, May 16, 2005

Women in the Nordic countries are most likely to be paid on a par with men and experience equal job opportunities, according to a global report released Monday. At the other end of the spectrum, Egypt, Turkey, and Pakistan have the widest economic gaps between men and women.

The World Economic Forum's report also singled out the United States for criticism, saying it lagged behind many Western European nations.

The report used criteria including equal pay for equal work and female access to the labor market to rank 58 countries—all 30 OECD nations and another 28 emerging markets—on a "Gender Gap Index."* It also examined the representation of women in politics, access to education and access to reproductive health care.

No country on the list managed to close the gap entirely, the Swiss-based think tank found.

"Gender inequality is one of the most prominent examples of injustice in the world today," said Augusto Lopez-Claros, WEF Chief Economist and author of the report.

Lopez-Claros said that women continue to be discriminated against, often on the basis of cultural, religious, and historical beliefs, and countries that fail to close the gender gap do so at their own risk.

"Countries that do not fully capitalize on one-half of their human resources are clearly undermining their competitive potential," he said.

Lopez-Claros said the priority for closing the gap should be improving education prospects for women. Countries that do so benefit from falling adolescent pregnancy, greater income generation, and associated overall wealth generation, he said.

"The education of girls is probably the most important catalyst for change in society," he said.

The report found that Sweden, Norway, Iceland, Denmark, and Finland were best at narrowing the gap and providing a workable model for the rest of the world.

---

* For the complete list of rankings in the Gender Gap Index, see the Appendix.

It noted that Nordic countries are characterized by strong liberal societies, government transparency, welfare systems, and wide access for women to education, political, and work opportunities.

Lopez-Claros pointed out that women hold 45.3 percent of seats in the Swedish parliament, compared to a global average of female representation of 15.6 percent.

The United States, the world's largest economy, was ranked 17th [see the chart in the Appendix]. Lopez-Clarez said the ranking was low compared to much of Western Europe because of a lack of maternity leave benefits, high young female unemployment compared to young male unemployment, high adolescent fertility and low representation of women in politics—women hold just 14 percent of seats in Congress, less than the global average.

In Europe, non–European Union Switzerland scored relatively badly at number 34. It got a good rating on health and political empowerment, but fared less well on equal pay and women in the work force.

Italy and Greece have the worst rankings in the EU, at 45 and 50 respectively, mainly because of women's lack of decision-making power and poor career prospects.

In Asia, China was the highest-rated country at number 33, scoring well on economic participation but badly on education and political empowerment. Japan is a few places behind at 38.

New Zealand, Canada, the United Kingdom, Germany, and Australia rounded out the top 10 performers, while Pakistan, India, Mexico, Brazil, Greece, and Venezuela completed the bottom 10.

More Women Are Entering the Global Labour Force Than Ever Before, But Job Equality and Poverty Reduction Remain Elusive

INTERNATIONAL LABOUR ORGANIZATION, MARCH 5, 2004

Women are entering the global labour force in record numbers, but they still face higher unemployment rates and lower wages and represent 60 per cent of the world's 550 million working poor, says a new report by the International Labour Office (ILO) prepared for International Women's Day.

At the same time, a separate updated analysis of trends in the efforts of women to break through the glass ceiling says the rate of success in crashing through the invisible, symbolic barrier to top managerial jobs remains "slow, uneven and sometimes discouraging."

"These two reports provide a stark picture of the status of women in the world of work today," says ILO Director-General Juan Somavia. "Women must have an equal chance of reaching the top of the jobs ladder. And, unless progress is made in taking women out of poverty by creating productive and decent employment, the Millennium Development Goals of halving poverty by 2015 will remain out of reach in most regions of the world."

"Global Employment Trends for Women 2004," an analysis of female employment, says more women work today than ever before. In 2003, 1.1 billion of the world's 2.8 billion workers, or 40 per cent, were women, representing a worldwide increase of nearly 200 million women in employment in the past 10 years.

Still, the explosive growth in the female workforce has not been accompanied by true socio-economic empowerment for women, the report said. Nor has it led to equal pay for work of equal value or balanced benefits that would make women equal to men across nearly all occupations. "In short, true equality in the world of work is still out of reach," the report adds.

The study found that while the gap between the number of men and women in the labour force (the sum of the unemployed and employed) has been decreasing in all regions of the world since 1993, this decrease has varied widely. While women in the transition economies and East Asia—where the number of women working per 100 men is 91 and 83, respectively—have nearly closed the gap, in other regions of the world, such as the Middle East, North Africa, and South Asia, only 40 women per 100 men are economically active, the report says.

In the developing countries, women simply cannot afford to not work.

Meanwhile, female unemployment in 2003 was slightly higher than male unemployment for the world as a whole (6.4 per cent for female, 6.1 per cent for male), the ILO said, leaving 77.8 million women who were willing to work and looking for work without employment. Only in East Asia and sub-Saharan Africa did the regional male unemployment rate exceed that of women, with 3.7 per cent male unemployment in East Asia, compared to 2.7 per cent female unemployment, and 11.8 per cent unemployment for men in sub-Saharan Africa, compared to 9.6 per cent female unemployment.

In Latin America and the Caribbean, the female unemployment rate was 10.1 per cent compared to the male rate of 6.7 per cent, while in the Middle East and North Africa the female unemployment rate of 16.5 per cent was 6 percentage points higher than that of men. For young people in general, but specifically for young women aged 15–24 years, the difficulty in finding work was even more drastic, with 35.8 million young women involuntarily unemployed worldwide.

In the developing countries, women simply cannot afford to not work, the report says, noting that low unemployment rates thus mask the problem. The challenge for women in these countries is not gaining employment—they have to take whatever work is available and are likely to wind up in informal sector work such as agriculture with little, if any, social security benefits and a high degree of vulnerability—but in gaining decent and productive employment, the report says.

What is more, of the world's 550 million working poor—or persons unable to lift themselves and their families above the USD 1 per day threshold—330 million, or 60 per cent, are women, the report says. Adding the 330 million female working poor to the 77.8 million women who are unemployed means that at least 400 million decent jobs would be needed to provide unemployed and working poor women with a way out of poverty.

"Unless progress is made to take women out of working poverty by creating employment opportunities to help them secure productive and remunerative work in conditions of freedom, security and human dignity and thereby giving women the chance to work themselves out of poverty, the Millennium Development Goal of halving poverty by 2015 will not be reached in most regions of the world," the report says.

The report also found that women typically earn less than men. In the six occupations studied, women still earn less than what their male coworkers earn, even in "typically female" occupations such as nursing and teaching.

"Creating enough decent jobs for women is only possible if policy makers place employment at the centre of social and economic polices and recognize that women face more substantial challenges in the workplace than men," says Mr Somavia. "Raising incomes and opportunities for women lifts whole families out of poverty and it drives economic and social progress.

Women's Pay

Why the Gap Remains a Chasm

BY AARON BERNSTEIN
BUSINESS WEEK, JUNE 14, 2004

During the heyday of the women's movement more than 30 years ago, "59 cents on the dollar" was an oft-heard rallying cry, referring to how little women earned compared with men. Those concerns seem outdated today, when it's easy to find female doctors, lawyers, pop stars, even Presidential advisers. The progress toward equality in the workplace also shows up in government data on wages, which pegs women's average pay at 77 percent of men's compensation today.

But there's new evidence that women's advances may not be quite so robust after all. When you look at how much the typical woman actually earns over much of her career, the true figure is more like 44 percent of what the average man makes. That's the conclusion of a new study by Stephen J. Rose, an economist at Macro International Inc., a consulting firm, and Heidi I. Hartmann, President of the Institute for Women's Policy Research in Washington.

Why the big discrepancy? The Bureau of Labor Statistics (BLS) numbers, published every year, are accurate as far as they go. But they only measure the earnings of those who work full-time for an entire year. Only one-quarter of women, though, achieve this level of participation consistently throughout their working lives. So Rose and Hartmann looked at the pay of all men and women over 15 years, including those who worked part-time and dipped in and out of the labor force to care for children or elderly parents. This long-term perspective still shows an arc of progress: The 44 percent, based on average earnings between 1983 and 1998, jumped from 29 percent in the prior 15 years. But the more comprehensive view gives a less rosy picture of women's position in the work world.

Outright discrimination against women probably accounts for only about 10 percentage points of the pay gap, according to numerous studies. The bulk of the problem, then, lies with the conflicting needs and norms of society and employers. A majority of men and women still work in largely sex-segregated occupations, Rose and Hartmann's study shows, leaving many women stuck in lower-paying jobs such as cashiers and maids.

Family responsibilities, too, typically still fall more heavily on women, and neither society nor employers have found good ways to mesh those with job demands. Rose and Hartmann's data show that women can get equal treatment today—but mostly when they behave like traditional men and leave the primary family responsibilities at home. For the majority who can't or won't do that, the work world remains much less accommodating. Of course, many women choose to take time off or to work part-time to be with their children rather than stay on the job. Yet that choice itself is constrained by the widespread lack of day care and flexible job options, Hartmann argues. "The 44 percent gap we found shows that there are still tremendous differences in how the labor market treats men and women," she says.

> *One surprise was just how many women work most of their adult lives.*

Hartmann and Rose came to their results by examining long-term earnings trends. The 77 percent figure comes from the BLS's 2002 earnings survey and looks at how much full-time, year-round workers make in a given year. By contrast, Rose and Hartmann used a University of Michigan survey that has tracked a sample of randomly chosen people and their children since 1968. They looked at how much each person made between 1983 and 1998 in every year from age 26 to 59 (to exclude students and retirees).

One surprise was just how many women work most of their adult lives. Fully 96 percent of these prime-age women worked at least one of those 15 years, and they clocked an average of 12 years on the job. In other words, few women these days drop out altogether once they have kids.

But those few years out of the labor market carry a stiff penalty. More than half of all women spent at least a year out of the labor force, the study found, and they earned an average of $21,363 a year over the years they worked, after inflation adjustments, vs. nearly $30,000 for women who stuck with it for all 15 years. Indeed, anyone who drops out risks derailing their career and permanently slashing their pay. Just one year off cuts a woman's total earnings over 15 years by 32 percent, while two years slice it by 46 percent and three by 56 percent, according to Hartmann and Rose. The work world penalizes men nearly as much; their average pay drops by 25 percent if they take off a year. Fewer than 8 percent of men did so, however. "Our economic system is still based on a family division of labor, and women pay the price," says Rose.

Women also take a big hit for going part-time. On average, they work a lot less than men: 1,498 hours a year, vs. 2,219 worked by the typical man. The fewer hours women work account for about half of the total pay gap between the sexes, Rose and Hartmann concluded. Some women have turned to self-employment as a way to fit work and family together. But they often must accept lower pay in the process. Brita Bergland, a Windsor (Vt.) resident, found it difficult to manage her sales job at a printing company while she also cared for her aging mother and her daughter. So she struck out on her own six years ago and has managed the work-life balance much better ever since. The cost: about a $15,000 cut in annual earnings, down from the $55,000 to $60,000 she made as an employee. "These

> *Historical patterns of sex segregation remain strong across much of the economy.*

are the choices women make because society doesn't help them to support children and parents," says Bergland, who's now 50.

And while many women have made great strides in some highly visible professions such as law and medicine, historical patterns of sex segregation remain strong across much of the economy. Overall, just 15 percent of women work in jobs typically held by men, such as engineer, stockbroker, and judge, while fewer than 8 percent of men hold female-dominated jobs such as nurse, teacher, or sales clerk. These findings were reiterated in a detailed BLS analysis released on June 2 that uses the 2000 census to look at the jobs men and women hold.

Such a sex-segregated economy leaves women with some startling disadvantages. Overall, they earn less than men with the same education at all levels. Incredibly, male dropouts pulled down an average of $36,000 a year between 1983 and 1998, after inflation adjustments, while women with a bachelor's degree made $35,000. Women with a graduate degree averaged $42,000, but men got nearly $77,000.

The good news is that the pay gap continues to narrow no matter how it's measured. That's likely to continue; female college graduation rates surpass those of men, and they're catching up in grad school, too, so they're likely to gain from an economy that rewards skill. Women also should benefit from the ongoing shift to services, where they're more likely to work, and lose less than men from the decline of factory jobs.

Still, speedier progress probably won't happen without more employers making work sites family-friendly and revamping jobs to accommodate women and men as they seek to balance work and family demands. "The workplace needs to change to match the workforce," says Ellen Bravo, national director of 9to5, National Association of Working Women. Until that happens, a woman's labor will continue to be worth a fraction of a man's.

Employed, Yes—But Precariously

BY OXFAM INTERNATIONAL
FROM THE REPORT *TRADING AWAY OUR RIGHTS: WOMEN WORKING IN GLOBAL SUPPLY CHAINS*, 2004

Lucy, a Kenyan mother of two, sews the pockets onto children's jeans destined for Wal-Mart in the United States, the world's most successful retailer. Her factory, based in an export processing zone (EPZ) outside Nairobi, receives erratic, sub-contracted orders and must keep costs low and output high. Early in 2003, when her manager demanded she work non-stop for two days and nights to meet the shipping deadline, her partner walked out, leaving Lucy to raise the children, aged two and 13. "He said he will come back when the condition of my work is good." she said, "Till today the condition is becoming worse."

In May Lucy sold her table, cupboard, and bed so that she could pay the rent. Then she sold the cooking stove to buy her son's school uniform. In June, when orders stopped for eight weeks, so did the pay. Her parents, living in a village 150km north of Nairobi, agreed to take her children, and she has not seen them for six months. "If this EPZ could be better, and consider us as people, and give us leave and holidays, then I would be able to go and see the children," she said.

Production targets are unrealistically high, and Lucy is expected to put in extra hours to meet them. In September she worked 20 hours of overtime but was paid for only six. Talk of trade unions is banned, and the factory atmosphere is intimidating. "Supervisors abuse us . . . If we talk, they say, 'Shut your beak. Even a child can do your job.'" She most pities the young female helpers doing the low-skill tasks such as counting and cleaning the garments. "If you are a helper, you need security," she said. "They are sexually harassed to keep their job. That's why as women we are so oppressed. Because you can't secure your job through the trade union, you have to buy it with sex."[1]

Lucy depends on this job. But she and her family should not be forced to pay such a price to keep it. Worldwide, working women like her—making garments, cutting flowers, and picking fruit—are demanding their fair share of the gains from trade. The only asset they have to offer in trade is their labour. This makes a critical test for globalisation: can it create jobs that empower, rather than undermine, women as workers? So far it is failing.

Facing Precarious Employment

The last 20 years of trade liberalisation have certainly created jobs for millions of women workers, who occupy 60 to 90 per cent of jobs in the labour intensive stages of the clothing and fresh-produce global supply chains. And these jobs are desperately needed by women and their families. "May God bless the flowers, because they provide us with work," say the women working in Colombia's flower greenhouses.[2] "Even though the salaries are low," said Ana, working in a maquila, or export-assembly factory, in Honduras, "the maquilas give us employment—they help us to make ends meet."[3] Facing school costs and medical expenses, poor families increasingly depend on earning cash incomes to meet their most basic needs. Many hope to escape rural poverty, migrating across provinces and countries to do so. And the crisis of HIV and AIDS makes some families all the more dependent on those who can work, increasing the need for their caring work too.

> *Precarious employment is far from new—it has long been the reality for poor people, especially in informal sectors in developing countries.*

For many individual women, their jobs have brought economic independence, greater equality in the household, and personal empowerment. But the past 20 years have also witnessed the emergence of a new business model . . . based on companies outsourcing production through global supply chains that demand low-cost and "flexible" labour. In many countries, national labour laws have been weakened or not enforced to accommodate these demands. As a result, millions of women and men at the end of those supply chains are employed precariously:

- insecure: on short-term contracts with limited access to social protection

- exhausted: through working long hours at high pressure in unhealthy conditions

- undermined: in their attempts to organise and demand for their rights to be met.

Precarious employment is far from new—it has long been the reality for poor people, especially in informal sectors in developing countries. Export-sector jobs, connecting them to some of the world's most profitable companies, should be an opportunity for more secure and empowering employment. But instead, the sourcing and purchasing practices of those companies create pressures down the chain which result in precarious conditions. The impact falls on poor communities in rich countries, too, where workers employed in trade-competing sectors—often migrants and immigrants—likewise face precarious conditions. The result is a two-tier labour market, split between those whose standard of living grows with the economy and those employed precariously without minimal protection.

All poor people face costs when employed in this way, but the impacts fall particularly hard on women:

- Women typically have less education, land, or savings than the men in their families. That weaker negotiating position leaves them with the primary responsibility for caring work in the home—raising children, tending to the sick and elderly—and it makes them more dependent on whatever paid work they can get. No wonder they occupy the vast majority of jobs at the end of global supply chains.

- Stuck in low-skilled, low-paid jobs, women are less able to renegotiate their household roles, and so they bear a double burden of paid and unpaid work. That undermines their struggle for greater equality in the home and in society, and leaves little time for participating in workers' organisations and social support groups.

- Insecure contracts often lack the protections and benefits—such as limits on overtime, rest days, sick leave, accident cover, and maternity leave—that are invaluable for women in supporting their families. Without this support, either from the State or from employers, the strain often undermines their own health and well-being and their children's futures.[4]

The harmful impacts of precarious employment can be long-term and community-wide. And they are felt in every country. Women and migrants from poor communities in rich countries also face precarious terms of employment in trade-competing sectors. The pressure of competition from low-cost imports is clearly one reason—but so too is the pressure inherent in being employed in a global supply chain, whether it is sourcing domestically or overseas.

Permanently Temporary

Women are more likely than men to be hired on short-term, seasonal, casual, or homework contracts, renewed every year, every three months, or even every day. They end up working long-term but without the protection and support that come with long-term jobs. In Chile and South Africa, women get the temporary jobs in the fruit sector, hired on "rolling contracts" for up to 11 months, year after year. "We are permanent when it suits management," as one South African woman put it.[5] Likewise, almost all of China's migrant garment workers are given one-year contracts, repeatedly renewed, leaving them with no job security.

It is sometimes assumed that women want such "flexible" jobs so that they have time to care for their families. When those jobs are well protected under law, women can benefit from having this choice. But for the vast majority of women interviewed, working on short-term contracts is not a choice but a necessity—and is all that they are offered. For home-based workers in the UK (of whom 90 per cent are women and 50 per cent are from ethnic minorities), the supply of work they receive from manufacturers is highly irregular, sometimes with very short deadlines. "Homeworkers often get no redundancy pay, holiday or sick pay, and no pension," said Linda Devereux, Director of the National Group on Homeworking. "This is not the kind of 'flexibility' that any woman worker is hoping for."[6] The increasing use of temporary and contract labour is a worrying trend in many countries.

Employed: But Who Is the Employer?

When workers are not formally recognised as employees, they fall outside the protection of labour law. In some countries, having no written contract means having no legal recognition. In Bangladesh, only 46 per cent of women garment workers interviewed had the letter of employment that is needed to establish the employment relationship. No wonder that almost none received pay slips or was enrolled in a health scheme, and the vast majority got no paid maternity leave.[7] Layers of supply chain sub-contracting can blur legal relationships too. In Chile, companies are liable in law if the sub-contractors they use fail to pay sub-contracted workers' wages or benefits—but the law is not always enforced. "In many cases the company has kept on workers who have not been paid by the farm labour contractor," explained Jessica, hired through a contractor to pack grapes for export to the USA. "The company tells them 'But we have paid for all that—it is the farm labour contractor who has not fulfilled his obligations to you.'"[8]

Little Support for Families

Paid maternity leave is essential for supporting women as workers and as mothers—and for ensuring the health of the current and future workforce. But women hired on short-term contracts who become pregnant simply do not get their contract renewed, and others with the right in law often cannot claim it in practice. In Kenya, some garment workers seek back-street abortions, losing the baby and risking their own lives in order to save the job. And those who do have children pay the price. "In my company you lose your work number when you go on maternity," explained one young woman. "This means that, if you are lucky enough to be readmitted, you come back as a new employee, losing all the benefits for the period worked before going on maternity leave."[9]

Stuck at the Bottom

In the fruit industry, women are the pickers, sorters, graders, and packers. In the flower industry, they do the weeding, plant tying, pruning, cutting, picking, and packing. In the garment industry, women sew, finish, and pack the clothes. There is skill in doing these jobs fast and well, but they are perceived to be low-skill—and similar to women's tasks at home—so are typically low-paid. Supervisors, machine operators, and technicians tend to be men, earning more. In Colombia's flower farms, for example, technical irrigation systems are managed by men; irrigation with a hose is women's work.[10] Dividing men's and women's roles in this way not only entrenches pay gaps but also reinforces women's subordination. One route to getting better-paid and more secure jobs is training, but few women are ever offered the chance. "[The farmer] only chooses the men for training," said one South African fruit picker. "Here it is not a woman's thing, it is a man's thing. You remain a general worker, even though you have the knowledge."[11]

Low Pay, High Pressure

Minimum wage levels in many countries are scarcely more than poverty wages—set by what the market will pay, not what families need. As a result, women often cannot earn enough in a basic week's work. In Honduras, garment workers earn above the minimum wage, but the government's own calculations show that the minimum covers only 33 per cent of a family's basic needs.[12] In Bangladesh, 98 per cent of garment workers interviewed were paid at least the minimum wage—but its level was set in 1994, and the price of basic foods has more than doubled since then. Allowing for inflation, one woman in three is effectively earning below the minimum.[13]

Workers in every country studied reported extreme pressure to work harder, faster, and longer. An array of targets, incentives, and penalties are used to raise workers' productivity. Piece-rate pay—a fixed amount paid for each piece of clothing stitched, or each kilogram of grapes picked—is increasingly common. In Chile, one in three fruit pickers and packers paid by piece-rate earned the minimum wage or less. And they put in extraordinary hours to make it, facing an average workweek of 63 hours, sometimes up to 18 hours a day.[14] In the UK, manufacturers provide homeworkers with assembly kits that they say will take 14 hours to complete—but homeworkers report that they actually take 40. And they can legally be paid only 80 per cent of the minimum wage to do it. Under pressure from homeworkers' organisations, trade unions, and some high-street retailers, the UK government has at last committed itself to ending that legal exemption by April 2004.[15]

Kenyan garment workers commonly face penalties for lateness and mistakes, and charges for medical treatment. It can add up to more than a month's earnings. "We've heard from many workers who have been charged and fined by their employers," said Steve Ouma, Senior Programme Officer at the Kenyan Human Rights Commission. "Instead of getting a payslip at the end of the month, they got a bill—and it was deducted from next month's pay. It's outrageous that workers are forced to subsidise production this way."[16]

Long Overtime at Short Notice

Overtime is voluntary by law, but for many women workers it is a condition of employment and imposed at short notice. In China, overtime is legally limited to 36 hours per month, but in Guangdong province the vast majority of workers surveyed across seven factories faced more than 150 extra hours each month.[17] One "workers' handbook" in Shenzhen stipulated that "When workers cannot do overtime they have to apply to the supervisors for a written exemption from overtime."[18] Some factory managers compel workers to put in long hours by setting basic wages at a low level. "I don't like doing overtime," said Seetha, sewing garments in Sri Lanka, "but if I don't, then I won't have enough money. So we are forced to do overtime."[19] By law in most countries, overtime hours should be paid at a premium—but in reality, workers are often robbed of their rightful overtime earnings.

Banned, Bullied, and Broke: Troubles Organising

> *I used to think that the union was not important but after I got involved and met workers and unions in other factories, I realised how important it is to protect workers' rights. If a worker has a problem, they don't know what their rights are. The union can advise them and help solve it. I have gained lots of experience and now I know about the law. If I don't use it to help the workers, who will?*—Prem, a union committee member in a Thai factory producing for Banana Republic and Polo Ralph Lauren

In 2003, Prem's union succeeded in stopping the factory from hiring new workers on repeated provisional contracts and was seeking ways to support sub-contracted workers who are banned from joining the union by management.[20]

The freedom to join trade unions is fundamental for workers to improve their own working conditions. Unions represent their members on issues ranging from health and safety to salaries and working hours. They work both through formal "collective bargaining" with employers and by assisting individual workers, for example, in cases of unfair dismissal or sexual harassment. They lobby national governments and international institutions to ensure that workers' concerns are reflected in national and global policy making. For decades, trade union struggles and solidarity have been central to securing and strengthening workers' rights worldwide.

But unions face heavy restrictions, in law or practice, in many countries. Employers' tactics of intimidation, firing, and physical violence are exacerbated when governments fail to step in. And the transformations taking place in global labour markets pose an additional challenge. Traditional union members—male, long-term employees based in close-knit workforces—are rapidly being replaced and outnumbered by young, female, temporary workers in a migratory workforce with no history or culture of union involvement and little time to go to meetings. When the workforce is so fragmented, and if the legal employer's identity is blurred, the challenge to create a recognised, powerful voice for workers is huge.

Given the low incomes of their members, and the decline in their traditional member base, many unions do not have the resources to respond. Workers earning barely more than poverty wages may be reluctant to pay monthly dues, especially if they are often more afraid of losing their jobs than hopeful of winning better conditions. It creates a vicious circle: those workers most in need of collective support are the least likely to be recruited.

Raising women's participation is a key priority for many unions, but some still face barriers. "The trade union helps us with many problems," said one South African fruit picker, "and shop stewards show respect when we discuss problems with them."[21] But other

---

Raising women's participation is a key priority for many unions, but some still face barriers.

---

workers were cynical, saying, "Seasonal workers get very little or no opportunity to speak to the farmer. The union represents only permanent workers."[22] And in one Kenyan EPZ, women account for three out of four workers, but only one in five union representatives. Why? Union recruitment there often takes place in bars in the evening—places not considered appropriate for women. And issues of high importance to women, such as maternity leave and protection from sexual harassment, have not yet been raised in industrial-court disputes.[23]

Many unions are tackling these problems by joining forces with women workers' organisations, recruiting female organisers, setting up women's committees, and campaigning on women workers' concerns. By 1998, for example, more than two-thirds of the International Confederation of Free Trade Unions' national centres and more than half of affiliate unions were promoting the issue of women in leadership roles. They promoted action such as guaranteeing reserved and additional seats for women, and setting targets for gender balance.[24] And in the late 1990s, a network of its African affiliates launched initiatives to integrate gender perspectives throughout their member unions' work.[25] New national alliances are also forming. In Sri Lanka, for example, several trade unions and non-government organisations have recently joined forces as the Labour Rights Core Group, to campaign on critical issues facing women workers in the garment industry such as living wages, freedom of association, and compensation for impending job losses.

Sexual Harassment

Many women interviewed said sexual harassment was a commonplace abuse of power in the workplace. Yet it often goes officially unreported, due to fear or a sense of futility. From Honduras and the USA to Morocco and Cambodia, women workers reported cases of male supervisors demanding sexual favours in return for getting or keeping jobs. Long shifts to meet deadlines put women's safety at risk. "We are very afraid of being harassed or raped by gangsters, because we often have to work late at night and walk home in the dark," said one young worker in Cambodia.[26] Persistent harassment drives some women to leave their job, at the risk of not finding another. For Hasina, a former garment worker in Bangalore, India, the only alternative was to turn to sex work. "You are subjected to all kinds of sexual harassment in the factory," she said. "Supervisors, production managers, and watchmen touch you without giving you anything in return. In this job, at least you are paid for the same."[27]

Hidden Costs Beyond the Workplace

Away from the factory floor and beyond the farm gate, precarious employment has long-term and community-wide costs. When women are employed without security and with minimal support from employers or the State, they bear the burden, often at the cost of their own health or their families' future, creating a long-term liability for society.

Children: The Price Paid by the Next Generation

"We are here for production, not reproduction," declared a Kenyan garment factory manager who refuses to provide paid maternity leave or childcare facilities.[28] This attitude may suit the short-term needs of his company. But when workers cannot care adequately for themselves or their children, the development prospects of the country are damaged.

Visit a garment workers' dormitory and you will occasionally see, pinned to the wall, a photograph of a small child. Nid, working in a garment factory in Bangkok, Thailand, has one of her son. He is two, and she left him with her parents in their village eight hours away, because there is no childcare provided at work. She sees him every three months, and is forced to take three days' unpaid leave for the journey there and back.[29]

Working women can be forced to consider extreme solutions to childcare problems. In one fruit-growing valley in British Columbia, Canada, one in three women fruit pickers—mostly Punjabi immigrants—take their young children with them to the farms, because of a lack of alternatives.[30] Even when childcare is available, arrangements can be extreme: one nursery school teacher in Colombia described flower workers dropping their children off at the nursery at four in the morning and picking them up at ten at night.[31]

> *Working women can be forced to consider extreme solutions to childcare problems.*

School-aged children, too, often pay the price. Some working mothers can only cope with their double duties by taking their eldest daughters out of school to look after younger children, but the girls lose their chances of a more skilled job in the future. In Morocco, 80 per cent of women with older children had taken daughters under 14 out of school to do so—no wonder that many eventually follow their mothers into the factories.[32] School-going children are sometimes drawn into helping with their parents' work in order to meet production targets, even in rich countries. One school in the UK raised concerns that pupils who were children of homeworkers were neglecting their own homework (school work) in order to help their mothers meet their production targets.[33]

Long-term Ill-health

Unhealthy working conditions mean that workers face medical costs, and their working lives may be cut short. Pesticide use on farms has an appalling history in some countries. A decade-long U.S. medical study found that members of California's United Farm Workers organisation had elevated rates of leukemia and cancers associated with pesticide exposure.[34] A study conducted in a hospital in Rancagua, Chile, between January and September 1993 found that all 90 babies born with neural defects were children of temporary fruit workers.[35] Procedures have improved on some farms in the past decade, but in 2000, 62 per cent of female Chilean grape pickers surveyed reported being in contact with pesticides while working in the fields, while fewer than half of all agricultural workers there have occupational insurance coverage.[36]

Less dramatic but more common are low-level illnesses and injuries. Fruit and flower pickers and packers from Colombia, Chile, the USA, and South Africa commonly reported headaches, respiratory problems, and eye pain from handling pesticides. Garment factory workers from Bangladesh to Morocco commonly suffer headaches, coughing, vomiting, fever, and physical exhaustion. Poor ventilation in lint-filled rooms can lead to debilitating respiratory diseases. Hired in jobs that demand highly dexterous and repetitive movements, many women suffer joint injuries and back, leg, and shoulder pain.

Health and safety legislation may fail to prevent or recognise these illnesses specific to new industries and to women. Sri Lankan occupational health law recognises only gas-related respiratory diseases, not those caused by the fabric lint inhaled by thousands of garment workers, leaving those affected with no legal recourse.[37] U.S. pesticide exposure standards are based on the adult male body, ignoring the higher risks for pregnant female agricultural workers, such as spontaneous abortion and structural birth defects.[38]

Workers often foot the bill for their workplace illnesses. "When we get sick, we're the ones who have to pay the doctor," said Zineb, sewing clothes in Morocco for El Corte Inglés and other Spanish retailers. "We don't have the right to get sick—they punish us if we do."[39] In Colombia, some women flower workers pay for health coverage that they never get. "The employers deduct social security contributions," said one, "but when we go to the doctor, they say that the employer is not up to date or that we don't even appear in the system."[40] Rokeya, a Bangladeshi garment factory worker, was ill at work for two months before she missed a day to go to the doctor. Her manager then deducted two days' pay, and she lost her full attendance bonus. On return she was told to work an extra eight hours unpaid to catch up with her target. In total, being unwell cost her 11 days' wages.[41]

Challenges in the Home

When women start contributing to household income, the household balance of power may be challenged, particularly with male relatives.[42] Some women find their status in the household improves. "My family treat me better than before," said one young Cambodian woman now employed in the garment industry. "I used to be scolded or beaten, but not any more, because now the family miss me and receive the money I send home."[43] Some women are able to play a bigger role in decision making and decide how to use their own earnings—but others face serious drawbacks. Earning an income can result in less financial support from other household members, especially from the fathers of the women's children, leaving them no better off overall and more dependent on keeping their jobs.[44] Women's employment may provoke violence from husbands and male relatives, who themselves may be out of work. In Bangladesh, garment workers reported facing threats and suspicion from their husbands when they arrived home at two in the morning, especially when their employers—hiding evidence of excessive overtime—had punched their official hour cards to show that they left the factory at six in the evening.[45]

Little Change in Caring Work

When employed in short-term and unstable jobs, women are not in a strong position to re-negotiate their care-giving responsibilities at home. As a result, most continue to be the primary carers, with little or no support from their partners. In Colombia, women working long hours on flower farms are still expected to do almost all the housework: they report their husbands helping with less than 10 per cent of the time taken in childcare, less than 5 per cent of cooking, and 1 per cent of cleaning.[46] Likewise, in Bangladesh, women garment workers are still four times more likely than their husbands to be responsible for looking after sick children and dependants.[47]

Lose a Community—Gain a New, but Transient, One

When women migrate for work, they often lose their ties with their traditional communities which had provided support such as childcare, informal credit, and neighbourhood security. As migrants, many face language and social barriers. In Cambodia the social stigma attached to young single women who have lived outside family control makes life difficult for them, even on brief visits home. "Garment workers are not considered good women for marriage," explained one. "In some cases engagements were broken off because the woman was a garment worker."[48] Likewise, flick through the pages of a Sri Lankan newspaper and you will see marriage advertisements that say "Garment women, please do not reply."[49]

The loss of traditional support systems and poor prospects for marriage on returning home make women workers more dependent on new networks with fellow workers—a fragile dependency, given that their jobs are transient and unstable. Angela, sewing garments in a Kenyan factory, expressed frustration at her isolation from the wider community: "It is not possible to do anything else. There is no time to take care of your own children, visit people, do business or go to college. Even going to church has become a problem . . . We are somehow isolated."[50]

Trading Away Workers' Rights

These harsh realities experienced by women workers provide eloquent testimony of a model of globalisation that is failing poor people. Over the past 20 years, while investors' rights have been deepened and extended through international trade agreements, workers' rights have moved in the opposite direction. In the absence of global institutions that are widely trusted and empowered to underpin these rights in the global economy, many governments have been trading them away. In law and in practice, they have eroded employment security, benefits, and protections in order to provide the flexibility demanded in global supply chains. But the short-term gains of this strategy can come at the cost of a long-term liability for society—and women workers are paying the heaviest price.

Notes

1. G. Sayer (2003)

2. B. Herrera et al. (2003)

3. J. Ramsey (2003) "Improving Labour Rights for Women Maquila Workers," Oxford: Oxfam GB

4. Based on D. Elson (1999) "Labour markets at gendered institutions: equality, efficiency and empowerment issues," *World Development* 27(3), and M. Williams (2003) *Gender Mainstreaming in the Multilateral Trading System*, The Commonwealth Secretariat: London

5. Women on Farms (2003)

6. National Group on Homeworking (2003), and Oxfam interview November 17, 2003

7. A. Barkat et al. (2003)

8. CEDEM (2003)

9. P. Kamungi and S. Ouma (2003)

10. B. Herrera et al. (2003)

11. Women on Farms (2003)

12. K.A. Ver Beek (2001) "Maquiladoras: exploitation or emancipation? An overview of the situation of maquiladora workers in Honduras," *World Development* 29(9)

13. A. Barkat et al. (2003)

14. D. López (2003)

15. National Group on Homeworking (2003)

16. Oxfam interview November 10, 2003

17. Liu, K.M. (2003)

18. Pun, N. (2003)

19. Centre for Policy Alternatives (2003)

20. Oxfam interview 2 July 2003

21. S. Smith, D. Auret, S. Barrientos, C. Dolan, K.Kleinbooi, C. Njobvu, M. Opondo, and A. Tallontire (2003) "Ethical Trade in African Horticulture: Gender, Rights and Participation," Institute of Development Studies, Sussex. Preliminary report for multi-stakeholder workshop, June 26, 2003

22. Women on Farms (2003)

23. P. Kamungi and S. Ouma (2003)

24. International Confederation of Free Trade Unions(2003) "Discussion Guide," 8th World Women's Conference, Melbourne, Australia, February 18-21, 2003

25. ILO "Promoting Gender Equality," Booklet 6: "Alliances and Solidarity to Promote Women Workers' Rights," ILO: Geneva

26. Womyn's Agenda for Change (2002) "A Social Study of Women Workers in the Cambodian Garment Industry," *www.womynsagenda.org*

27. N. Pandey (2003) "Case Study on Female Garment Workers in Bangalore," Hyderabad: Oxfam GB

28. P. Kamungi and S. Ouma (2003)

29. Oxfam interview December 9, 2002

30. G. Moher (2003)

31. V. Meier (1999) "Cut-flower production in Colombia: a major development success story for women?" *Environment and Planning* 31: 273–89

32. Colectivo Al Jaima and La Chabaka (2003)

33. National Group on Homeworking (2003)

34. P.K. Mills and S. Kwong (2001) "Cancer incidence in the United Farm Workers of America (UFW) 1987–1997," *American Journal of Industrial Medicine* 40: 596–603

35. Green (1995) cited in S. Barrientos, A. Bee, A.Matear, and I. Vogel (1999) *Women and Agribusiness: Working Miracles in the Chilean Fruit Export Sector*, Basingstoke: Macmillan

36. Riquelme (2000) cited in CEDEM (2003)

37. Centre for Policy Alternatives (2003)

38. Solomon (2000) cited in Goldstein and Leonard(2003)

39. Colectivo Al Jaima and La Chabaka (2003)

40. B. Herrera et al. 2003

41. A. Barkat et al. 2003

42. D. Elson (1999) op. cit.

43. Womyn's Agenda for Change (2001) op. cit.

44. N. Folbre (1994) *Who Pays for the Kids? Gender and the Structures of Constraint*, London: Routledge

45. A. Barkat et al. (2003)

46. V. Meier (1999) op. cit.

47. A. Barkat et al. (2003)

48. Womyn's Agenda for Change (2002) op. cit.

49. Centre for Policy Alternatives (2003)

50. P. Kamungi and S. Ouma (2003)

II. Women's Health Care
and Mortality

Editor's Introduction

A round the world women suffer from poorer health and higher rates of disability and mortality than men. Biologists will tell us there should be a natural preponderance of women in any population, but in many areas of the world, particularly in North Africa and Asia, men outnumber women. In a 1990 essay for the *New York Review of Books*, Nobel Prize–winning economist Amartya Sen claimed that Asia's population should have 100 million more women than it does. Though a recent study has cast some doubt on the accuracy of this number, there is no denying that, in comparison with men, many women suffer from unequal care in health, medicine, and nutrition, due largely to the social and economic disparities discussed in the first chapter of this book. In the 1970s, during the second wave of feminism in the United States, feminists who were dissatisfied with the care they were receiving from male physicians started educational campaigns and published books—such as the landmark *Our Bodies, Ourselves* (1969)—to empower women by educating them about their own bodies. Still, numerous barriers to achieving equality of health remain, particularly for women in developing nations. Most notably, women in poorer countries suffer a far higher maternal mortality rate—which could easily be prevented if women were offered prenatal care and proper nutrition. A recent UNICEF report addresses the situation:

> How can such a heavy burden of death, disease, and disability have continued for so long with so little outcry? In part, the conspiracy of silence surrounding [maternal mortality] is a reflection of the fact that women are conditioned not to complain but to cope. . . . As one midwife puts it: "If hundreds of thousands of men were suffering and dying every year, alone and in fear and in agony, or if millions upon millions of men were being injured and disabled and humiliated, sustaining massive and untreated injuries and wounds to their genitalia, leaving them in constant pain, infertile, and incontinent and in dread of having sex, then we would all have heard about this issue long ago and something would have been done."

In the first article of this chapter, "Modern Asia's Anomaly: The Girls Who Don't Get Born," Celia W. Dugger suggests that the phenomenon Sen identified can be attributed in part to sex-selective abortions. Even before the introduction of ultrasound technology, daughters suffered because of the traditional preference for sons; many girls were the victims of infanticide or neglect. The author believes that economic modernization may help to weaken the patriarchal family structure, thereby reducing the number of sex-selective abortions.

The next article, "Fighting the Silent Epidemic," is an interview with Joy Phumaphi, the assistant-director general of the Family and Community Health Cluster at the World Health Organization. Phumaphi discusses the estimated half million mothers and 11 million children who die of mainly preventable causes every year. To reduce these numbers, she argues, more women need access to professional health care.

In "Women, Inequality, and the Burden of HIV," Bisola O. Ojikutu and Valerie E. Stone describe an alarming increase in the number on every continent of women infected with HIV. The spread of HIV among women is the result of biological and sociopolitical factors. According to the authors, women's inequality—their limited education, lack of access to health services and economic opportunities, and subservient social position—directly contributes to their higher infection rate.

In "Working for Women's Sexual Rights," Barbara Crossette examines the efforts of advocates such as Dr. Nafis Sadik, executive director of the United Nations Population Fund, who have transformed the debate over how to cut population growth into a campaign to assure that women have the right to control their own sexuality. She has encouraged developing nations to look at family planning in terms of what would best aid their development and has cast culturally contentious practices, such as female circumcision, as public health issues.

Modern Asia's Anomaly

The Girls Who Don't Get Born

By Celia W. Dugger
The New York Times, May 6, 2001

Women are making strides in both India and China, which together are home to a third of humanity. They are living longer and are more likely to be able to read and write than ever before. In democratic India, more than a million women have been elected to village councils in the past decade.

Yet, despite this progress, female fetuses are being aborted at startling rates in China and across broad swaths of India, new census data shows. As the population of girls relative to boys has tumbled in northern and western India over the past decade, these regions have begun to catch up with China's dismal statistics. The spread of ultrasound technology in these societies, with their strong preferences for sons, has made it easy to find out the sex of a child before birth and to abort unwanted daughters.

But why is this bias against girls so pronounced in large parts of South and East Asia when it is not in many other regions of the developing world? What is it about China and these areas of India, with their radically different histories and forms of government, that explains this terrible convergence? And why, even now, don't the women themselves—more likely than ever before to be literate—insist on giving birth to their girls?

Economists and demographers are beginning to grapple with these questions and say there are likely to be many complex factors at play. But some think the answer lies in a particular form of patriarchal family, common in most parts of both regions. In such families, the daughter's responsibility to care for her parents largely ends at marriage, while the son's lasts for life. And in India and China, where there is still no universal, government-sponsored social security system, the question of who supports aging parents is very important, these researchers say.

"The grown woman can be useful," said Monica Das Gupta, a demographer at the World Bank in Washington who has co-written papers on this subject. "She can work in the fields and be a good mother, but the fact that she's educated and employed doesn't change her value to her parents, who won't benefit from all that."

Intriguingly, Ms. Das Gupta, who studied family patterns across the developing world, says that in sub-Saharan Africa, Latin America, and Southeast Asia, daughters and sons share the job of caring for their aging parents—and in these regions the sex ratios are normal.

In most parts of both India and China, where more than two billion people live, it is generally a son who carries on the family line, inherits ancestral land, cares for his parents as they age, and performs the most important ceremonial roles when they die. In India, the son lights his parents' funeral pyres, helping set their souls at peace. In China, he cares for his parents' spirits in the afterlife so they do not wander for eternity as hungry ghosts.

In contrast, a daughter in either society typically leaves her natal family after marrying to become part of her husband's family, moving in with them and tending to her in-laws. "There's a traditional expression used in China," said Li Shuzhuo, director of the Population Research Center at Xian Jiaotong University in Xian, China. "Daughters are like water that splashes out of the family and cannot be gotten back after marriage."

> *"The woman realizes that her value goes up with the birth of sons and down with daughters."*— Jaswinder Kaur, a women's health worker

Before ultrasound, girls were sometimes victims of infanticide, but much more commonly they were victims of neglect—not fed as well as boys or taken to the doctor as quickly. But the advent of sex-selective abortions has added a new and definitive means for acting on a prejudice against girls—and statistics reflect the results, experts say.

Normally, women around the world give birth to 105 or 106 boys for every 100 girls. But according to China's latest census, there were 117 boys born for every 100 girls in 2000, up from 114 in 1990.

And in India, the early 2001 census data show that in the north and west, which include some of the richest states, the ratio of girls to boys, from birth to age 6, has declined sharply in the same decade. In Punjab the rate has fallen to 793 girls per 1,000 boys from 875; in Rajasthan from 915 to 865; in Gujarat from 928 to 878; and in Maharashtra from 946 To 917. The overall rate in India fell from 945 to 927.

Discrimination faced by girls both before and after birth has contributed to the fact that 50 million to 80 million more girls and women might have been alive today in India and China, according to demographers and economists, had they received treatment equal to that of boys and men.

Each country has its own policies or customs that may well have intensified the problem. In China, pressure to abort girls has been increased by family planning rules that limit couples to one or two children. In India, the sizable dowries that families pay to get daughters married add to the financial burden of raising girls. But in both societies, Ms. Das Gupta and Professor Li maintain in a paper they co-wrote, the kind of patriarchal family system prevalent in much of India and China is the root of the preference for sons, who are needed to provide security for parents in old age. It is a theory that echoes in the words of ordinary people in Punjab, India's richest agricultural state.

"The boy is like the lamp of the family, and everybody wants it lit continuously," said Jaswinder Kaur, a women's health worker in Daffarpur. "The woman realizes that her value goes up with the birth of sons and down with daughters."

India and China both prohibit sex-selective abortions, but the practice is hard to police since the pregnant women and those who perform the abortions have every incentive to keep the secret. But the numbers from the new census have drawn wide attention in India. Some officials are saying the law must be more stringently enforced; women's advocates call for a social movement against customs like dowry.

The high priests of the Sikh religion recently announced that anyone who becomes a *kudi-maar*—daughter-killer—will be excommunicated. Punjab, which now has the lowest proportion in the nation of young girls to boys, has a large Sikh population.

The experience of South Korea suggests that urbanization, modernization, and rising prosperity may help loosen the bonds of traditional family life, said Minja Kim Choe, a demographer at the East-West Center in Honolulu. Figures there, she says, show the ratio there seeming to peak in 1990 at 117 boys per 100 girls and declining to 110 by 1999. While that's still high, it is better, she said. South Korea's economic transformation, she believes, is gradually weakening the patriarchal family system as people become more independent economically and socially from their families.

But China and India are still mainly agrarian societies, and it is likely to be a long time before these lumbering behemoths can hope to see such benefits.

Fighting the Silent Epidemic

THE WORLD HEALTH ORGANIZATION, APRIL 7, 2005

Joy Phumaphi (48), is a former health minister and former member of parliament of Botswana. She has a B.Com and a Masters in finance accounting and decision sciences. She also serves as a commissioner on the U.N. Secretary-General's Commission on HIV/ AIDS and Governance in Africa. Before that, she served as a member of the U.N. Reference Group on Economics and a member of the United Nations Development Programme (UNDP) Advisory Board for Africa. Phumaphi was appointed as WHO's Assistant Director-General for Family and Community Health in August 2003.

An estimated 11 million children under five years and more than half a million mothers globally are likely to die this year due largely to preventable causes. As Assistant Director-General of the Family and Community Health cluster at WHO, Joy Phumaphi's task is to raise the profile of perhaps one of the most neglected areas of public health. Phumaphi told the Bulletin *she hopes the* World health report 2005: Make every mother and child count, *to be published on 7 April, and the recent appointment of Ethiopian fashion model Liya Kebede as WHO's Goodwill Ambassador will spur efforts to do more for maternal and child health.*

Q: What simple, cost-effective treatments if introduced in the world's poorest countries could substantially improve the survival chances of mothers when they give birth?

A: Access to professional care in the pregnancy, childbirth, and post-partum periods is key to addressing the major causes of maternal mortality. If comprehensive services were made available, you could save most of the lives of the mothers who die. Often, women who haemorrhage badly need a blood transfusion and often don't have access to a hospital. Obstructed labour is also a problem and facilities that can provide caesarian section are often not accessible. Many women deliver in unsafe conditions with traditional birth attendants who do not have the skills needed to help when something goes wrong. In addition, sepsis or infection can occur, so making antibiotics available to health services would also save lives. Women need skilled antenatal care to identify whether there is a need for delivery in a health facility. Antenatal care providers can show women how to look after themselves during pregnancy and deal with any serious health problems that may arise.

Q: What other factors can contribute to the ill health of mothers and neonates?

A: There are aggravating conditions where there is a high prevalence of HIV/AIDS, or malaria. That's why it's so important for services for the prevention of mother-to-child transmission of HIV to be made available and for women to be given a prophylaxis for malaria during pregnancy and assisted to have a balanced diet to be as healthy as possible during pregnancy.

Q: What simple interventions could save newborn infants' lives?

A: If comprehensive health services with skilled professionals are accessible during pregnancy, birth, and afterwards, then a very large proportion of newborn lives can also be saved. As newborn mortality is a substantial part of overall child mortality, it needs to be tackled.

Q: Have you given your cluster a new direction since you arrived at WHO in August 2003?

A: The cluster deals with primary health-care programmes in the most basic developing country health systems. The tools, guidelines, norms, and standards that have been developed over the years are very good. But now we need to increase support to help countries translate this into policies, strategies, and practices. We have created a new department, Making Pregnancy Safer, and strengthened an existing one, Gender, Women, and Health. This shift in focus should put us in a better position to attain the Millennium Development Goals on maternal and child health.

Q: What concrete progress in improving maternal and infant survival do you expect from World Health Day on 7 April, when the world health report devoted to the subject will be launched?

A: Every year we lose about 11 million under-fives, mainly to preventable causes. Four million of these under-fives die in the first week of life. An additional 3.3 million die during or before birth. Every year, about 529,000 women die during pregnancy, childbirth, or shortly afterwards. These are alarming statistics; it's a huge loss of life. But the scale of the problem and the scale of neglect in this area are not yet apparent to the global community. It is a silent epidemic.

We hope to give a voice to the 11 million children and half a million women we are losing every year. These women and children are not dying in a natural disaster, like a tsunami. It is a disaster which the adult world can prevent because we have the solutions.

Q: And what are those solutions?

A: Children die from pneumonia and from sepsis, but we have the antibiotics to treat these. Many are still dying of diarrhoeal disease, but oral rehydration salts (ORS) are an effective treatment, and were developed decades ago. We know that breastfeeding is the best form of nutrition for babies and that it also protects them from illness. We know that kangaroo mother care, when the baby is strapped to the mother, is the best way to care for small or premature babies. We have interventions, like the Integrated Management of Childhood Illnesses. We have evidence-based solutions which the World Health Day and the World health report should publicize to the global community. However, to make these solutions work for women and babies we need skilled professionals with the drugs, supplies, and equipment to implement them.

> *Often, women and children are the first to suffer when the access to health-care services is disrupted.*

Q: Which countries have the highest mortality rates for mothers, infants, and children?

A: The Democratic Republic of Congo, Ethiopia, and Nigeria have the highest death rates in Africa for mothers and children. Every year, 136,000 maternal and more than 1.1 million newborn deaths occur in India alone. Some countries which dealt consistently with these challenges and made progress in the 1990s have now regressed due to HIV/AIDS and depressed economies, such as Malawi, Mozambique, Zambia, and Zimbabwe. Middle-income countries, such as Botswana, Namibia, and South Africa are also experiencing setbacks and need mainly guidance on policy-making.

Q: The health of mothers, infants, and children is particularly vulnerable in conflict situations and emergencies; how are you tackling this problem?

A: Often, women and children are the first to suffer when the access to health-care services is disrupted. We work with WHO's Health Action in Crisis (HAC) when they support and set up emergency medical care facilities. Usually, these address communicable diseases and injuries and, if we are lucky, mental health issues. In order for them to save mothers and children, they must include routine antenatal care, skilled care at every birth with back-up services for women with complications. Care must continue after delivery for the mother and infant and appropriate service links must be made with child care and family planning services. These services must be available from day one.

Q: More than 500,000 women are dying in childbirth every year; has this situation got worse in the last 50 years, or was it even worse before?

A: In the last 50 years it has definitely improved but it has more or less remained stagnant in the past 10 years because the issue is not being given enough attention. Recently, the Kenyan parliament was given statistics on the number of women dying in childbirth in their country and they were shocked. They did not understand why so many women should still be dying in childbirth. This came to light in Kenya when we launched a training programme called Beyond the Numbers, which helps countries document the causes of maternal death, count the women who die in childbirth, and establish ways to bring the right solutions to communities. Often the policy-makers are not aware of the numbers because a lot of women deliver at home, die at home, and are not being counted.

Women, Inequality, and the Burden of HIV

By Bisola O. Ojikutu, M.D., M.P.H., and Valerie E. Stone, M.D., M.P.H.
New England Journal of Medicine, February 17, 2005

Driving through KwaZulu-Natal, South Africa, one is struck by the lush farmland and beautiful coast. Beyond this panorama, however, lie rural communities such as Umbumbulu, with its unemployment rate of 60 percent and rampant violence, where 40 percent of women seeking prenatal care are positive for the human immunodeficiency virus (HIV).[1]

Thandi Dlamini (not her real name) grew up in a crowded four-room house in Umbumbulu with 13 family members. As the youngest girl, she was charged with cooking, cleaning, and caring for her elders. At 19 years of age, she met her first boyfriend. From the perspective of Thandi and other women in her community, he was quite a catch—he was older, unmarried, and financially stable. She dreamed that one day he would offer to pay her *lobola* (bride price) and she would have her own home. Several months after meeting, he and Thandi had sexual intercourse. Thandi says this was her first sexual encounter.

Nine months later, she gave birth to a daughter, Zama. The baby had many episodes of bloody diarrhea and uncontrollable vomiting. By six months of age, Zama was clearly failing to thrive, and Thandi consented to have her tested for HIV. When the young mother returned to the hospital for the results, she was given three tragic pieces of information: she had given her daughter HIV, no treatment was available, and Zama would not live long.

Ichilo. Disgrace. *Amahloni.* Shame. This is how Thandi describes her feelings after leaving the hospital. She didn't really know what HIV was, except that it caused people to speak in hushed tones. It took months for Thandi to tell her boyfriend. Soon after hearing the news, he disappeared. Shortly after that, Zama died.

Around the same time, 9000 miles away in Denver, a 32-year-old black woman was sharing Thandi's fate. In 1991, Donna Williams (not her real name) went to her doctor because of fatigue and consented to an HIV test. Weeks later, two women from the Denver Public Health Department arrived at her apartment. They informed her that she was HIV-positive and that her only option was to go to a specialty clinic at the public hospital. When she overcame her initial shock and went to the clinic, she was confronted by a sea of faces unlike her own—almost all men, many appearing near death. Terrified, she fled. A year passed before she obtained care for HIV.

Like Thandi, Donna grew up in a crowded home where she was the primary caregiver at a young age. Her mother had a series of abusive boyfriends, and in an effort to escape, Donna married an older man when she was 17 years old. During their first year of marriage, he was a good provider. Then his addiction to heroin surfaced and quickly destroyed their lives. For the next five years, he was in and out of prison, leaving his wife with their four children, unstably employed and transiently housed. After finally leaving her husband in 1987, Donna discovered that he was dying of AIDS. At the time, she was not sick and was struggling to survive as a single mother, so she did not get tested for HIV until 1991.

The differences between these two women are relatively few: native language, ethnic background, and land of birth. The list of similarities is substantially longer. Both are mothers and caregivers and both are poverty-stricken, transiently employed, and struggling to obtain basic daily requirements such as adequate housing. Both have had limited access to health care. Both have been dependent on men at some point in their lives for financial security. And all these similarities have contributed to their deadliest bond: HIV infection.

The legion of women with HIV infection now numbers in the millions. According to the World Health Organization, 19.2 million women were living with HIV or AIDS by the end of 2003.[2] An alarming increase in the number of women infected has been noted on almost every continent. The region that has been hit the hardest is sub-Saharan Africa, where 57 percent of infected persons are women. In the United States, HIV infection has begun to spread disproportionately among women of certain racial and ethnic groups. About 80 percent of all women living with HIV or AIDS in this country are members of a minority groups—66 percent are black, and 14 percent are Hispanic.[3] Globally, most women have acquired HIV through heterosexual intercourse.

Biology provides a partial explanation for women's increased risk of becoming infected with HIV. It is well established that during unprotected sex, HIV is transmitted more efficiently from male to female than from female to male. The mucosal lining of the vagina provides a more permeable membrane than does the penile shaft, and microlesions in the vaginal mucosa caused by other sexually transmitted infections permit increased viral penetration.[4]

However, the spread of HIV among women has sociopolitical as well as biologic roots: it arises from the inequity between the sexes, societies' class structures, and the inaccessibility of health care. In many societies, educational and employment opportunities for women are limited. Throughout the world, women are placed in subservient positions and lack the freedom to ask questions or to demand the use of condoms. In most societies, if a woman chooses to remain single, she is choosing a life limited by poverty and instability.

Inequality between the sexes is not unique to the non-Western world. In the United States, sex-based income inequity has fueled disproportionate rates of poverty among women, and women's options are limited as a result. Poor women, regardless of their nationality, share a fear of losing a male partner if it also means the loss of financial security. Thandi articulated it best when, in a discussion of sexual relationships with men, she noted that for many women, "it's either that or nothing." When "nothing" means not being able to afford food or shelter for themselves or their children, there really is no choice.

Both these women's stories demonstrate that HIV is one small piece of a larger puzzle. As these pieces multiply and shift, health care needs are often low on the priority list. Donna is thankful that none of her children have HIV, but she has had to help each one through tumultuous circumstances. Currently, she is supporting her daughter through recovery from drug addiction. At 46, she has custody of her 5-year-old granddaughter. She is unemployed and recently had to move back to a subsidized housing project because of her limited income. Through all these difficulties, her adherence to her regimen of highly active antiretroviral therapy has been sporadic. Consequently, she has been hospitalized four times for pneumonia in the past two years.

After Zama's death, Thandi gave birth to a second daughter—who is also HIV-positive. Luckily, through the support of a benefactor, this child has access to the same medications that would be used to treat her in the United States. Thandi's life revolves around ensuring that her daughter takes her medications and stays well. Her greatest concern is that she and her daughter will never have financial security. She is training to become an HIV counselor because she would like to help other women obtain and benefit from HIV treatment, but she has no income and is therefore still dependent on a boyfriend for support.

The lives of these and many other women with HIV infection are mired in adverse circumstances. HIV adds to the overwhelming burden that they must bear. Here in the United States, there are disparities between the sexes in the care received for HIV infection[5]— partly because of the complexity of these women's lives, but also because they are frequenty uninsured or underinsured and because they are often forced to seek care in systems that are not structured to meet their needs. For example, many HIV clinics have inflexible and inconvenient hours, long waiting times, and few staff members from the same racial or ethnic groups as the patients.

As antiretroviral medications become more widely available in the developing world, a major challenge will be finding ways not simply to dole out medications but also to simultaneously address the broader context. In both Thandi's world and Donna's, cultural, economic, and social structures must be changed to allow women more viable life options, Throughout the world, physicians can assist in this process by advocating a multidisciplinary approach to treatment and prevention that would address women's life circumstances along with their medical needs. Only when such change has been effected will HIV-infected women be able to obtain and benefit optimally from appropriate treatment, and only then will uninfected women be able to protect themselves from HIV infection and secure their own well-being.

Notes

1. 2004 Report on the global AIDS epidemic: 4th global report. Geneva: Joint United Nations Programme on HIV/AIDS (UNAIDS), 2004:22–58.

2. Ibid.

3. HIV/AIDS surveillance report. Vol. 15. Atlanta: Centers for Disease Control and Prevention, 2004:18–9.

4. Padian NS, Shiboski SC, Glass SO, Vittinhoff E. Heterosexual transmission of human immunodeficiency virus (HIV) in northern California: results from a ten-year study. Am J Epidemiol 1997;146:350–7.

5. Shapiro MF, Morton SC, McCaffrey DF, et al. Variations in the care of HIV-infected adults in the United States: results from the HIV Cost and Services Utilization Study. JAMA 1999;281: 2305–15.

Working for Women's Sexual Rights

By Barbara Crossette
The New York Times, October 2, 2000

When Nafis Sadik, an obstetrician from Pakistan, was hired by the United Nations Population Fund more than 20 years ago, family planning in the developing world was largely something bureaucrats foisted on poor women who were targets for meeting fertility-control quotas.

"The world has come very far since then," said Dr. Sadik, who, by 1987, had become the fund's executive director. Quotas and targets are gone. So is some of the squeamishness about sex. And "population control" is no longer an acceptable description of what family planners do.

Dr. Sadik, who will retire at the end of the year, has presided over a social revolution. Working with independent family planning organizations, women's groups on every continent, and many governments, she and other increasingly powerful women in the United Nations system have turned the debate over how to cut population growth into a campaign for women's rights.

Other women involved in this process include Carol Bellamy, the executive director of Unicef, the children's fund; Noeleen Heyzer of Unifem, the United Nations' development organization for women; and lately Gro Harlem Brundtland, director general of the World Health Organization.

The United Nations itself is now in new territory, supporting the concept that women should have the right to make their own decisions about bearing children, and that they should have access to education and health services, a range of family planning tools, and, as a last resort, safe abortions.

"If women had the power to make decisions about sexual activity and its consequences," says the new annual report of the population fund, "they could avoid many of the 80 million unwanted pregnancies each year, 20 million unsafe abortions, some 750,000 maternal deaths and many times that number of infections and injuries."

"They could also avoid many of the 333 million sexually transmitted infections contracted each year," says the report, titled *Lives Together, Worlds Apart: Men and Women in a Time of Change*. The report says that the needs of women are often "invisible to men" and that until discrimination against women ends, the world's poorest countries—where women are also often the most oppressed—cannot develop to their potential.

Here are some of the statistics from the report:

- One woman a minute dies of pregnancy-related causes.
- Sexually transmitted diseases afflict five times more women than men.
- An estimated two-thirds of the 300 million children without access to education are girls, and two-thirds of the 880 million illiterate adults are women.
- Ninety-nine percent of the approximately 500,000 maternal deaths each year are in developing countries.

The message that women must be able to make more decisions about their lives is not welcomed by every government and culture, and not only in the developing world or among Islamic nations. As the United Nations began to move in the mid-1980s toward more unambiguous support for women's rights, in which it included the right to seek a safe abortion, the American Congress dealt the population fund—which now has an annual budget of $250 million—heavy financial blows.

The message that women must be able to make more decisions about their lives is not welcomed by every government and culture.

In an interview, Dr. Sadik said her successor will have work to do, but at least will be able to do it in a new atmosphere of frankness.

"The most difficult issues of behavior or practices like rape, incest, female genital mutilation, the idea of female reproductive rights—all these concepts we would never have been able to discuss just a few years ago," Dr. Sadik said. That sexual violence, the sex trade, AIDS, and other issues like the need to provide adolescents with information and services to promote safe sex can be talked about openly in the United Nations and government offices "is an indication of massive, massive change in thinking," she said.

Many women's health experts say that the most significant shift of gears came at a 1994 conference in Cairo, which Dr. Sadik directed.

"Cairo represented a fundamental paradigm shift in the way the population field perceives the problem and, most important, the solution," said Adrienne Germain, president of the International Women's Health Coalition in New York, which assists women's health groups in the third world. "It put women's health and rights at the center of the agenda, recognizing that in so doing, demographic ends would also be served."

Dr. Sadik said she came early to her view that it was often pointless and inhumane to curb population growth by government edict.

"That came from my experience in Pakistan," she said. "When I worked in obstetrics, I found that when you told women, 'You must plan your next birth at least two years later,' they would say: 'Not for me. I must have a son.' They were so anemic, so ill—and yet they had no control over their lives.

"I remember making speeches in 1975 saying unless women had rights to control their own fertility they would have no other rights."

Dr. Sadik, 71, said her Muslim upbringing and her background in the developing world have enhanced her credibility in dealing with reluctant or suspicious governments and societies. She was born in 1929 in the Indian state of Uttar Pradesh, before the partition of British India in 1947 into Muslim- and Hindu-majority nations. She was educated in medicine and public health in Calcutta, Karachi, and at the Baltimore City Hospital and Johns Hopkins University. She still wears an Indian sari rather than a Pakistani shalwar-kamiz.

In her work, she has encouraged developing countries to look at population growth in connection with economic trends.

Dr. Sadik also has tried to avoid emotional debates over cultural values by casting practices like female genital mutilation—the cutting of all or part of female genitals, often in very young girls—a public health issue. "My view always is that culture and values are supposed to be helpful to societies," she said. "Not to discriminate. Not to subjugate. Not to perpetuate practices that are going to be harmful."

Among South Asians, the Pakistanis have been the least successful, she said, because a political commitment to family planning declined. And, she said, mullahs often swayed public opinion by speaking of using contraceptives as a sin or even by claiming that soap given to women to keep their bodies clean was laced with a sterilization agent.

The country's present military ruler, Gen. Pervez Musharraf, has asked for her advice. "I gave him a lot," she said emphatically.

III. Violence Against Women

Editor's Introduction

"**T**he majority of terrorists—and those against whom they are rebelling—are men," Robin Morgan writes in her 1989 classic *The Demon Lover*. "The majority of women, caught in the middle, want no more of this newly intensified old battle to death between fathers and sons. Always mothers, daughters, sisters, and wives are, in the words of an ancient Vietnamese proverb, 'the grass that gets trampled when the elephants fight.'"

Today, civilian deaths ("collateral damage") constitute nearly 70 percent of casualties in armed conflicts, and most of the victims are women and children. While they serve in ever increasing numbers in the armed forces, women still suffer most when civil society breaks down, living in constant fear of rape and abduction. According to Human Rights Watch, women in Baghdad have been living under virtual house arrest since the invasion and occupation of Iraq.

The greatest danger for most women, however, lies in the home; it is estimated that nearly a third of all women worldwide have suffered abuse at the hands of a male intimate. Domestic violence and sexual assault are global pandemics, affecting women of every culture, race, and class. Though social scientists and biologists may dispute what motivates an abuser or rapist, it is clear that women suffer violence due in part to their economic and political disempowerment. Domestic abuse and marital rape are still legal in many places. Even where they are considered crimes, women fear for their safety and reputation if they file a report with local authorities—who usually fail to convict offenders anyway. Furthermore, women, especially those with children, usually depend on a male wage earner and simply cannot afford to escape abusive situations in the home.

In "Rape as a War Crime," an uncredited author examines the long history of rape as a tactic in armed conflict. While rape was once considered a mere corollary of war, newly established criminal courts have recognized sexual violence as a crime against humanity. Still, cultural taboos prevent many women from speaking out against offenders, and little help is available for the victims who seek it.

Catherine Lutz and Jon Elliston examine the effects of armed conflict in Iraq and Afghanistan on the U.S. homefront in "Domestic Terror." American military officials deny that domestic violence is more common among military families than in civilian populations, but recent statistics and anecdotal evidence suggest that the partners of soldiers—particularly soldiers who have seen combat—are abused by their spouses more often. The abuse is often attributed to post-traumatic stress disorder, but the authors suggest that the abuse is caused by the desensitization to violence that soldiers undergo during their military training and on the battlefield.

In the following article, "For More Afghan Women, Immolation Is Escape," Carlotta Gall reports that women in larger Afghani cities have benefited from the fall of the Taliban—many are now in school or working—but nothing has changed for the women in rural areas. Traded between families like chattel, many are abused by their husbands and in-laws. The situation is so bad for some that they have taken to setting themselves on fire.

Even during times of peace, the threat of violence is often used to control women, particularly their sexuality. In "Honour Killings" Ahmar Mustikhan examines the traditional Pakistani practice of murdering female relatives who have shamed themselves or their families. While individuals carry out these murders, human rights activists note that the state is also culpable because it fails to prosecute offenders. In January 2005 President Pervez Musharraf signed a bill outlawing the practice of honor killing. Islamic laws, however, give the family of the victim the legal authority to forgive a murderer, and in the case of honor killings, they often do.

Rape as a War Crime

AMERICA PRESS, OCTOBER 13, 2003

Ethnic and regional wars, especially over the past two decades in Africa and the Balkans, have brought with them death and destruction on a massive scale. But these same destructive forces have also taken the form of widespread sexual violence as a deliberate strategy. In Sierra Leone, rape has been referred to as that country's silent war crime. There and in other regions marked by armed conflict, few perpetrators have been brought to justice because of an atmosphere of impunity. The situation has recently begun to change, however, because of newly established international criminal courts that recognize sexual violence as a crime against humanity.

The first such court to be established—through the United Nations Security Council—was the international criminal tribunal for the former Yugoslavia. It came into being in 1993 in The Hague in the Netherlands. A second was established a year later in Arusha, Tanzania, to consider war crimes committed in Rwanda. Both courts elevated the seriousness of rape to a crime against humanity as grave as murder. Their establishment, as well as the creation of a special court in Sierra Leone, has helped to solidify the legal basis for prosecuting rape and sexual violence as war crimes.

In Rwanda, the sheer scale of the sexual violence during a three-month period in 1994 led the international criminal tribunal for Rwanda to label it as genocide, in part because of its potential for spreading the virus that causes AIDS. According to a report published by Human Rights Watch, Hutu militia personnel and soldiers of the former government subjected thousands of Tutsi women to acts of sexual violence. One former Hutu official, Jean-Paul Akayesu, a mayor in the Taba commune, was tried by the court and found guilty of nine counts of genocide, crimes against humanity, and war crimes—including responsibility for rape. Women who had witnessed the rapes testified that he had stood by, allegedly saying to the rapists at one point: "Don't complain to me now that you don't know what a Tutsi woman tastes like." On his orders, the women who had been raped were killed the next day. Mr. Akayesu is currently serving a life sentence in Mali.

In The Hague, too, crimes of sexual violence have resulted in indictments and convictions. The violence included so-called enforced pregnancy, carried out by Serbian soldiers, with the intention that their victims bear Serbian babies. During NATO's three-month bombing campaign in 1999, Serb paramilitary troops and Yugoslav forces carried out acts of sexual violence against Albanian Muslim women. The repeated attacks in detention camps, homes, and barns were intended not only to terrorize, but also to extort money from families forced to flee their homes as part of the campaign of ethnic cleansing.

In what advocates view as a landmark decision, in February 2001 three Bosnian Serb soldiers tried in The Hague's war crimes tribunal were found guilty of mass rape and sexual enslavement. The three received a combined sentence of 60 years. Amnesty International—which, like Human Rights Watch, has denounced sexual violence as a war crime—called the verdict an important step for women's rights, because it demonstrates that sexual enslavement during armed conflicts can now be acknowledged as a crime against humanity and that perpetrators can be held accountable.

> *Because of social and cultural taboos, victims frequently shrink from speaking out.*

Difficult barriers to accountability remain, however. Because of social and cultural taboos, victims frequently shrink from speaking out, knowing that they may face rejection and even retaliation in their own communities. Nor, in the aftermath of mass violence of this kind, is much help available for victims. On a small scale, groups like Doctors Without Borders run programs that include measures to reduce the risk of H.I.V. infection. But the psychological consequences alone can be so devastating that some women have resorted to suicide. Government corruption and a lack of political will, moreover, present still other barriers to vigorous prosecution. Barriers notwithstanding, the recognition by the courts in The Hague and Arusha—as well as one in Sierra Leone—that mass rape as a war strategy can be punishable as a crime against humanity represents an important step toward vigorous prosecution of rape as a war crime.

But in other parts of the world the problem of impunity remains. Just this past March, Refugees International released a report titled *No Safe Place: Burma's Army and the Rape of Ethnic Women.* The report states that the Burmese military is using sexual violence—committed both by officers and soldiers—as a means of stifling dissent and destroying ethnic communities. With Burma's military government denying mass rape charges that even the U.S. State Department accepts as credible, the prospect of accountability remains a distant one there and in other parts of the world where armed conflicts continue.

Domestic Terror

When Several Soldiers Killed Their Wives, an Old Problem Was Suddenly News

BY CATHERINE LUTZ AND JON ELLISTON
THE NATION, OCTOBER 14, 2002

The crusty critic Paul Fussell observed that war is always ironic, because things always end up so far from the glory-trailing myths that help start them. Irony, though, pales beside the fear and anger that now swirl around Fort Bragg, North Carolina, the source of many of the troops sent to Afghanistan. It was there that four soldiers recently confused their wives for the enemy and killed them. Marilyn Griffin was stabbed 70 times and her trailer set on fire, Teresa Nieves and Andrea Floyd were shot in the head, and Jennifer Wright was strangled. All four couples had children, several now orphaned because two of the men shot themselves after killing their wives.

The murders garnered wide attention because three of the soldiers served in Special Operations units that have fought in Afghanistan, and because they clustered over a five-week period in June and July. The killings have raised a host of questions—about the effect of war on the people who wage it, the spillover on civilians from training military personnel to kill, the role of military institutional values, and even the possible psychiatric side-effects of an antimalarial drug the Army gives its soldiers. On the epidemic of violence against women throughout the United States and on the role of masculinity and misogyny in both military and civilian domestic violence, however, there has been a deafening silence.

Military officials have focused on marital problems and family stress, and have fiercely contested the notion that domestic violence is a more severe problem in the military than in civilian populations, although the Pentagon has not invested much in finding out what the comparison would look like. One Army-funded study that was done, however, found that reports of "severe aggression" against spouses ran more than three times higher among Army families than among civilian ones in 1998.

The military nonetheless maintains that violence against spouses is no more prevalent in the armed forces, arguing that it uses different criteria than civilian authorities for identifying domestic violence, including severe verbal abuse. "People have been throwing some wild figures around," says Lieut. Col. James Cassella, a spokesman for the Defense Department. "My understanding is that it's kind of an apples and oranges comparison." But the military's method may actually underestimate the problem, since it long ignored violence against a legion of nonmarried partners, an especially important omission, considering that one recent study found that single men represent nearly 60 percent of soldiers using a gun or knife in attacks on women. And there is no way to corroborate independently the figures the military releases on domestic violence cases that are handled through military judicial processes, since they are shielded, as civilian police records are not, from public view. Moreover, the cited studies did take into account the most important demographic differences—the apples and oranges—in military and civilian populations.

Mary Beth Loucks-Sorrell, interim director of the North Carolina Coalition Against Domestic Violence, a statewide umbrella group based in Durham, is convinced that women partnered with soldiers face disproportionate risks of domestic abuse, a conclusion reached through years of fielding reports from abused women (and occasion-

> *There is no way to corroborate independently the figures the military releases on domestic violence cases that are handled through military judicial processes.*

ally men). Just since January, she said, North Carolina's 100 counties have seen at least 40 men kill their partners, seven of them in Cumberland County, where Fort Bragg is located. Reports of abuse from military communities are not only more frequent, but the level of violence they describe is more extreme and, according to domestic violence groups, has become worse over the past several years. Soldiers also terrorize their partners in unique ways, reminding the women of the sniper and bare-handed killing skills they acquire in training.

On hearing of the four murders, many people in the general public and media asked whether the soldiers might have suffered from postcombat trauma or simply, as the military suggested, from the stress of deployment and its disruption of family life. Some commentators on the right went so far as to suggest that these killings are another kind of war casualty and give us one more reason for gratitude to U.S. soldiers. On the left, the combat-stress explanation can draw on the notion of the soldier as a victim of class violence and reluctant imperial tool. In both these views, the soldier's home-front violence is the traumatic outcome of "what he saw" in combat rather than the much more significant trauma of what he did.

Stan Goff, a Special Forces veteran of Vietnam and Haiti, and now a democracy activist in Raleigh, scoffs at the "TV docudrama version of war" underlying this assumption. "Go to Afghanistan," he says, "where you are insulated from outside scrutiny, and all the taboos you learned as a child are suspended. You take life more and more with impunity, and discover that the universe doesn't collapse when you drop the hammer on a human being, and for some, there is a real sense of power. For others, for all maybe, it's PTSD [post-traumatic stress disorder] on the installment plan." The effect of this sense of impunity was evident when a Special Forces soldier, who was once arrested for domestic violence, told one of us that Memorial Day ceremonies always left him pondering why he would get medals for killing others in battle but would be arrested if he killed his wife.

A distracting sideshow to the murder investigations has been a UPI report suggesting the soldiers might have suffered side-effects of Lariam, a drug the Army gives prophylactically to troops going to malarial areas. Prescribed for 22 million people since 1985, Lariam use is associated with vivid dreams, insomnia, and dizziness and is known to be correlated with neuropsychiatric problems in a tiny percentage of cases, found in one large study to be 1 in 13,000. (In the wake of Pentagon stonewalling on the health effects of anthrax inoculation and depleted uranium weapons, Defense Department denial that Lariam is a problem might justifiably be taken with a grain of salt, but the epidemiological numbers suggest that skepticism is warranted about the drug's relationship to domestic violence.) Nonetheless, the Pentagon has sent an epidemiological team to Fort Bragg to investigate this and other potential roots of the murders.

In the Pentagon's approach to the problem and in virtually all media accounts, gender has been left hidden in plain sight. As in the 1990s schoolyard shootings, where a rhetoric of "kids killing kids" disguised the fact that boys were overwhelmingly the killers, here the soldiers are seen simply as an occupational group and the problem, at most, as one of an institutional culture where soldiers have difficulty "asking for help" from family service providers abundantly available at installations like Bragg.

Not only does the military remain by reputation the most "masculine" occupation available, but people in Fayetteville and in the armed forces generally consider Special Forces and Delta Force, where three of the four men worked, the Army's toughest units. Special Operations units are some of the last in the military to exclude women, and they also specialize in unconventional warfare, which is combat that often follows neither the letter nor the spirit of the rules of war. As a sign in a Special Forces training area says: "Rule #1. There are no rules. Rule #2. Follow Rule #1." Such a macho, above-the-law culture provides not a small part of the recipe for domestic violence. Combine this with a double standard of sexuality, one in which, as many soldiers and their wives told us, some couples expect infidelity to take place on Special Forces deployments—where the men operate with unusual autonomy and are often surrounded by desperately poor women—whereas the infidelity of wives, reactive or not, real or imagined, can be punished with violence.

If there was a common thread that tied the murdered women's lives together, it was the one identified by Tanya Biank, a *Fayetteville Observer* reporter: All four of them had expressed a desire to leave their marriages, a situation that domestic violence workers have identified as the most dangerous time for women in abusive relationships. For that is when the control these men tend to insist on in their relationships appears about to dissolve. Christine Hansen is executive director of the Connecticut-based Miles Foundation, which has assisted more than 7,000 victims of military-related violence since 1996. Military personnel, she says, are controlled from above at work even more than most U.S. workers, and many come home looking to reassert control, often with violence. The anxieties about control, and consequently the violence, flare up most often before and after military deployments, Hansen says, as soldiers lose and then try to reinstate control. As the war in Afghanistan began last October, for example, "We could literally tell what units were being deployed from where, based on the volume of calls we received from given bases. Then the same thing happened on the other end, when they came back."

After the wave of murders at Fort Bragg, the Senate set aside money for a new Pentagon investigation of military domestic violence—the latest in a long line of commissions established over the course of the many gendered scandals of the past 10 years, from Tailhook to Aberdeen. Such investigations have neither stemmed the problem nor prompted the military to recognize the fundamental role of violent masculinity in crimes like the Fort Bragg killings. This would entail seeing the murders as a piece of the larger, epidemic problem of violent abuse by men within the military, including rape of female (and some male) soldiers and civilians, lesbian- and gay-bashing, and brutal hazing rituals, as Dorothy Mackey, director of Survivors Take Action Against Abuse by Military Personnel, a national network of counseling groups based in Ohio, points out.

Of the 1,213 reported domestic violence incidents known to military police and judged to merit disciplinary action in 2000, the military could report only 29 where the perpetrator was court-martialed or sent to a civilian court for prosecution. The military claims to have no data on the disciplinary outcome of the 12,068 cases reported to family services in that year. They also have no record of the outcome of 81 percent of the police cases. This poor record-keeping and apparent reluctance to prosecute offenders can be explained by the military's institutional interests in burying the problem of domestic violence. One such interest is public relations. To recruit and retain a force of 1.4 million, including women and married men, remains a monumental task that would only be made harder by widespread knowledge of the extent of the violence. Second, there are financial motives. Many soldiers cost more than $100,000 each to recruit and train, money that goes down the drain if a soldier is discharged or imprisoned. Finally, there is the continuing, if waning, power of a belief, still widespread in the prevolunteer and mostly unmarried force, that "if the Army had wanted you to have a wife, it would

Women have spoken out about the frequent failure of commanders to take their calls for help seriously.

have issued you one." Protecting women from domestic violence in this environment falls even farther down the list of missions to be accomplished than it does in the civilian sector.

The difficulties women have in leaving their abusers are well-known. Military wives have additional disincentives. The unemployment rate for military wives is extremely high—hovering around 20 percent for those living at Fort Bragg—and those who do find employment are often stuck in the minimum-wage retail jobs that are the main work available in the satellite economy around most large posts. If they report abuse, they risk not only retribution from their husbands, as do women in the civilian world, but loss of their total family income, health care and other benefits, and even their housing and neighbors if their husband is discharged. One Army program does provide $900 a month plus health care for the few abused women whose husbands are removed from the force for domestic violence. Fort Bragg has no domestic violence shelter, though for many years was donating a paltry $10 a day to a local shelter when military wives fled there.

Women married to abusive soldiers have been calling the Fayetteville newspaper and domestic violence shelters around the country in sharply higher numbers since the Fort Bragg killings were reported. According to advocates, many callers are terrified, fearing they will be next because of their partners' ongoing violence and death threats. Women have spoken out about the frequent failure of commanders to take their calls for help seriously. And they have complained that they were often sent to military chaplains, some of whom advised them that suffering is a woman's lot or that their husbands were just "working off some excess energy." One counselor at Fort Bragg was quoted in the *Washington Post* describing how she tells women to prepare their partners returning from deployment for changes they have made in his absence, like cutting their hair short: "He might be thinking about running his hands through that long, luxuriant hair," she said. "Don't surprise your husband." After the murders, rather than implementing new measures to protect the thousands of women already in its police and family advocacy files, in late August the military began to screen soldiers leaving Afghanistan for mental health problems. While this may not be a bad idea in general, it presumes that combat stress alone is what leads to domestic abuse, and creates the illusion that something is being done about domestic violence without addressing its fundamental causes.

The cultural celebration of soldiers, which has grown more fervent since the war on terror began, has hampered attempts to address the problem. In good times, critical views of military practice are not well received; in the new atmosphere of intimidation fostered by the Bush Administration since last September 11, they may be considered tantamount to treason. Christine Hansen, who has received death threats since her foundation appeared in news stories about the murders, notes that some civilian judges have been even more reluctant than before to convict soldiers of domestic violence, when doing so would trigger the Lautenberg Amendment, a 1996 law that prohibits convicted abusers from owning firearms. The idea that the soldier makes an unrecompensable sacrifice creates a halo effect, so that the murderers are painted as victims of the horrors of combat, while scant attention is paid to the women they killed or the system's failure to prevent their deaths. As Stan Goff told us, soldiers in this climate can turn to their wives and say, "The culture's worshiping me. Why aren't you?"

In a widely disseminated Pentagon directive issued last November, Deputy Defense Secretary Paul Wolfowitz declared that "domestic violence is an offense against the institutional values of the military." But domestic violence, rape, and male supremacism itself are not anomalies or sideshows to war; instead, they lie near the center of how it is prosecuted and narrated. The millions of women throughout the world currently threatened by soldiers will look to their advocates and each other for their ultimate safety, and may have a unique appreciation for the ironies of focusing on more abstract terrors when they face such immediate dangers so close to home.

For More Afghan Women, Immolation Is Escape

By Carlotta Gall
The New York Times, March 8, 2004

Waiflike, draped in a pale blue veil, Madina, 20, sits on her hospital bed, bandages covering the terrible, raw burns on her neck and chest. Her hands tremble. She picks nervously at the soles of her feet and confesses that three months earlier she set herself on fire with kerosene.

Beside her, on the next bed, her mother-in-law, Bibi Khanum, and her brother-in-law, Abdul Muhammad, 18, confirm her account but deny her reason, which Madina would explain only outside on a terrace, away from her husband's family. "All the time they beat me," she said. "They broke my arm. But what should I do? This was my home."

Accounts like Madina's are repeated across Afghanistan, doctors and human rights workers say. They are discovering more and more young women who have set themselves on fire, desperate to escape the cruelties of family life and harsh tribal traditions that show no sign of changing despite the end of Taliban rule and the dawn of democracy.

Doctors and nurses in Kabul and Jalalabad say they have seen more cases recently, partly because the population has been swollen by the return of two million refugees and because cases are being tracked for the first time by rights groups, hospitals, and the government.

But the trauma and social upheaval of decades of war, poverty, and illiteracy in Afghanistan have also intensified the traditional pressures on young women, they say.

The recently formed Afghan Independent Human Rights Commission recorded 40 such cases in just the past six months in Herat, a western city of half a million people.

Karima Karimi, one of the commission's officers, says she suspects that the actual figure is higher, and President Hamid Karzai has ordered an investigation. Officials at the commission said it was reasonable to estimate that Afghanistan had hundreds of such cases in a year.

"It is not only in Herat; it is in all of Afghanistan," said Dr. Soraya Rahim, deputy minister of women's affairs, on her return from a government investigative trip to Herat.

"It takes different forms in different provinces," she said in a telephone interview. "Some take tablets. Some cut their wrists. Some hang themselves. Some burn themselves.

"But the reason is very important. The first reason is our very bad tradition of forced marriage. Girls think this is the only way, that there is no other way in life."

Educated women in the cities who were repressed by the old Taliban government have benefited from the changes in Afghanistan, and many are now working and studying. But in villages and remote tribal areas, the new order has not improved women's long-standing low status.

Daughters are often exchanged between families, are given in marriage as compensation for crimes, or are married to men two or three times their age.

When young girls marry, they leave home to live with their husband's extended family, where the mother-in-law rules the household. Often they are seen as little more than a new source of labor.

The desperate attempts of young women to escape lives dictated by tribal customs and a deeply conservative Islam are undeniable.

While the authorities have little idea of the full extent of the burnings, because families hide them out of shame and often claim they are accidents, the desperate attempts of young women to escape lives dictated by tribal customs and a deeply conservative Islam are undeniable.

Often they resort to burning, since kerosene and cooking fuels are easily accessible to women. In heavily populated eastern Afghanistan, the chief of anesthesiology at Jalalabad's Public Hospital No. 1, Muhammad Naseem, said the hospital received an average of 20 burn cases a month, at least two or three of which were self-inflicted.

The rest were household accidents, most caused by pressure cookers, gas or oil stoves or kerosene lamps, which account for many more cases of burns to women and children than those that are self-inflicted.

Nurses often learn the difference only in moments of confidence, or they spot telltale signs of family problems, like the absence of hospital visits by the husband. For the first time, human rights officials are paying attention, too.

The tribal areas, populated by Pashtuns who live by a code entirely their own, are particularly harsh in their treatment of women, said Sharifa, an officer from the human rights commission in Jalalabad. Like many Afghans, she uses only one name.

She said that when she visited the women's wards of Hospital No. 1 one day last month, she found five women who had tried self-immolation. One morning at the hospital, one of the five died after suffering for 11 days.

Madina's account is typical of the hardships young women encounter. She was married at 15 in an exchange of daughters between two families, a common practice in Afghanistan. She married Din Muhammad, and his sister was married to her uncle.

Madina said she had borne two children—Najiba, 4, and Taj Muhammad, 2. When her husband was jailed for drug offenses three years ago, she moved back from Pakistan to live with her in-laws in the village of Charbagh, in eastern Afghanistan.

In the interview on the hospital terrace, Madina explained that her troubles began a year ago, when the girl who had married her uncle died during pregnancy. Madina's mother-in-law turned her grief on Madina. "She would say, 'My daughter is in the grave, and you are still alive,'" Madina recounted.

In the hospital room, her mother-in-law, Bibi Khanum, a small woman with blue eyes and tiny hands, denied driving Madina to try to kill herself.

"God knows if it was cruelty," she said. "The reason she was impatient was because her husband was in jail."

"It's not true," Madina whispered.

Madina's husband, freed from prison and remorseful, has promised to take her to live away from the rest of the family. They are poor, and she is painfully thin and ill, but recovering. Away from her mother-in-law, she does not tremble.

Qadri Gul, 20, one of Dr. Naseem's patients, was less fortunate, dying after 11 days. Married for five years, she was the mother of two children. Her husband took a second wife shortly after they had wed, and she told the hospital staff and her family that her husband and her in-laws had beaten her daily, and had even encouraged her when she had threatened to burn herself.

She visited her parents and her numerous sisters in Jalalabad for the Muslim festival of Id al-Fitr in November. "Her body was completely bruised," her sister Basmina recalled. "She had marks on her buttocks and said, 'I don't know if I will get better.'"

They did not tell their mother, who nevertheless sensed that all was not well. "She was upset," the mother, Bibi Jan, recalled. "She did not put henna on her hands. She looked unhappy."

She went home after the holiday with a toy car for her son, but when the children started fighting over it, she took it away. That sparked a fight with her husband. He slammed a glass into her head, knocking her out. When she regained consciousness, she threatened to kill herself by setting herself on fire.

"He laughed and said: 'There are the matches and the kerosene. Burn yourself,'" Basmina recounted.

As she lay dying in the hospital, Qadri Gul told her mother and sisters what had happened. Sharifa from the human rights office also interviewed her.

Her mother said: "She blamed her husband, her brother-in-law, and her mother-in-law. I will leave them to God, but I will just ask them the question 'What did you do to my daughter?'" She was sitting in her courtyard, surrounded by relatives and mourners on the third day after her daughter's death.

"She was a very good girl," her mother said. "From neck to legs she was burnt."

Honour Killings

Violence Against Women in Pakistan

By Ahmar Mustikhan
Canadian Dimension, February 1, 2000

At least 2,000 women die in the south Asian state of Pakistan each year for exercising the fundamental right to love. And according to the country's leading woman lawyer, Hina Jilani, "The right of life of women in Pakistan is conditional on their obeying social norms and traditions." A female stands condemned to instant death upon mere suspicion or allegation that she has had, or was about to have, extramarital sex.

The practice, called "honour killings," is most prevalent in the largely tribal provinces of Balochistan and the North West Frontier Province, bordering Iran and Afghanistan, respectively. The dark practice of honour killings is not limited to the tribal territories, however—it spills over into the towns and cities, as well. A report by the Human Rights Commission of Pakistan (HRCP) said at least 286 women were killed "for honour" in Punjab, a province long emancipated from the tribal code of conduct. In the more feudal-oriented southeastern Sindh province, nearly 200 girls and women were killed "for honour" in the first three months of 1999.

Strangely, in some districts if a woman or girl is even seen in the company of a stranger, it is assumed that the two were planning to have—or have had—sex, and she is killed. The male is also condemned, but generally succeeds in escaping death. Reuter Foundation scholar and social anthropologist Nafisa Shah has conducted extensive research on the subject over several years. Shah told of a case that happened in Larkana, home district of former premier Benazir Bhutto, where a 14-year-old boy and a 10-year-old girl were axed to death on suspicion that they had had sex. Shah reported: "The boy had been drying his sweat-moist shirt in the sun after taking his younger siblings to visit neighbours on a hot summer day. The young girl was resting on a *charpoi* (a string bed), nearby. The girl's elder brother mistook the situation and spread the rumour; a few days later, the children were killed."

London-based researcher Angelika Pathak of Amnesty International (AI) has followed up Nafisa Shah's pioneering work. In her report, entitled "Pakistan: Violence Against Women in the Name of Honour," Ms. Pathak writes: "Every year in Pakistan hundreds of women, of all ages and in all parts of the country, are reported killed in the name of honour. Many cases go unreported. Almost all go unpunished. The lives of millions of women in Pakistan are circumscribed by traditions which enforce extreme seclusion and virtually proprietorial control over women with violence."

Pathak believes that state indifference, discriminatory laws, and the gender bias of much of the country's police force and judiciary have ensured virtual impunity for perpetrators of honour killings. She adds, "In fact, more and more killings committed for other motives take on the guise of honour killings on the correct assumption that they are rarely punished—and if so, only lightly punished." Pathak cites a journalist in Larkana as saying, "Women in our society are killed like hens. They have no way to escape and no say in what happens to them."

The victim may be a wife, daughter, sister, mother, or grandmother, and the culprit who carries out the execution—"as the state looks the other way"—is the husband, father, brother, son, or any other blood relative. Besides girls who decide to have hubbies of their own choice and battered wives seeking divorce, equally vulner-

---

"Women in our society are killed like hens. They have no way to escape and no say in what happens to them."—a journalist in Larkana, Pakistan

---

able are women who become rape victims. Pakistani laws practically equate a rape victim with anyone practicing consensual adultery.

What lies at the root of honour killings? The answer is simple: women are perceived not as human beings but as commodities belonging to men. According to tribal traditions and feudal norms, the woman's body is a commodity owned by the male members of the family and even the suspicion of extramarital sex lowers its value.

Says Pathak, "Perceived as the embodiment of the honour of their family, women must guard their virginity and chastity. By entering an adulterous relationship, a woman subverts the order of things, undermines the ownership rights of others to her body and indirectly challenges the social order as a whole." She explains that a woman's physical chastity is of uppermost importance and she loses her inherent value as an object worthy of possession—and therefore her right to life—at the merest hint of illicit sexual interest.

Male possessiveness seems to have no limits. Nafisa Shah states that, in one remote district of Sindh province, "a man killed his wife after he dreamed of her having an 'illicit' relationship." What AI noted with particular concern was that male possessiveness did not extend merely to a woman's body and her sexual behaviour, but to all of her behaviour, including her movements, language, and actions. According to HRCP director I.A. Rehman, a woman was killed by her husband in Balochistan province on the grounds that she had gone to visit her family without seeking his permission.

Most honour killings, however, take place when a girl gets married, or wishes to get married, of her own choice. On Friday, November 5, 1999, 19-year-old Deeba Shah was allegedly shot dead at her home by her mother's brother, Sikandar, in a shanty area of Pakistan's commercial capital, Karachi. A week earlier, Shah had secretly married her neighbour, Urs Khaskheli. A day before her murder, Khaskheli sent her family a legal notice to allow Shah to go with him. Upon receipt of the notice, Shah's family asked her if it was true. She said yes. In less than 24 hours she was shot dead.

According to London-based civil-rights activist Mrs. Shaheen Burney, "The girl fell victim to the barbaric tribal custom even in the city of Karachi." It was all the more deplorable that police had failed to save the life of the girl, Burney said, since her husband had notified the local police official well in advance that Shah's family might kill her. But the police did not lift a finger.

Girls who manage to elope get killed later. Mostly their male family members drag them into lengthy court trials by charging them with *zina* (fornication). The prospect of such girls ever getting justice vanished two decades ago in 1979, when former dictator Gen Zia ul-Haq promulgated the controversial Zina Ordinance, which made fornication and adultery criminal offences punishable by flogging and stoning to death. This black ordinance is still in force despite years of women's struggle against it.

AI also reported the case of Sher Bano, who was arrested under the Zina Ordinance for eloping with a man she wanted to marry. Though under police guard, her brother shot her dead on August 6, 1997, as she emerged from the court hearing in Peshawar, capital of the predominantly tribal Frontier province. "Often women choosing their spouses are abducted and not heard of again, perhaps murdered with no questions asked and no police action taken," the report noted.

Another major category of victims is women who seek divorce from abusive husbands. One such high-profile case was the gunning down of Samia Sarwar, 29, of Peshawar on April 6, 1999. This occurred at the law office Hina Jilani in Lahore, hometown of ousted premier Nawaz Sharif. Incredibly, Sarwar's mother, herself a medical doctor, led the killer to her daughter on the pretext that she could not walk there on her own.

Between 1989 and 1995, Sarwar's husband routinely kicked and beat her. She separated from him in 1995 after he threw her down the stairs while she was pregnant. But her family thought a divorce would bring dishonour.

Then, when Sarwar's parents went for a spring pilgrimage to Mecca, she escaped to Lahore, where she sought refuge at a women's shelter run by Jilani and her sister, Asma Jehangir, former chairperson of the HRCP. The killer also fired at Jilani, who escaped injury.

Perhaps most obnoxious was the collusion of the state in the murder. Zohra Yusuf, former general secretary of the HRCP, told this writer, "Ousted premier Nawaz Sharif's brother, Shahbaz Sharif, who was himself the chief executive of the Punjab province where the killing took place, provided full protection to the killers. They were allowed to escape by road in the limousine of a member of Pakistan's upper house of parliament, Senator Ilyas Bilour. None of the killers have been arrested to date."

According to the U.S.–based Sisterhood Is Global Institute (SIGI), "The fact that no arrests have been made in this case illustrates the willingness of the Pakistani governmental authorities to grant impunity for the crime of 'honour killing.'" Following the murder, a member of the opposition Pakistan People's Party, Senator Iqbal Haider, moved a resolution against honour killings in the Senate

---

Women who are coerced into sexual acts are also deemed to have dishonoured the family. There is no shame for the rapist.

(Pakistan's upper house of Parliament, presently under suspension following the October 12 military coup). After several weeks of dilly-dallying, the resolution was rejected. "During the debate, some of the government senators said those campaigning against honour killings were jeans-clad women," implying Westernized women, detached from Pakistan's realities, said Nafisa Shah.

Another abomination is that women who are coerced into sexual acts are also deemed to have dishonoured the family. There is no shame for the rapist. But "A woman raped shames the community and dishonours the man," writes Shah in the Reuter Foundation's *Paper 100*. In the same paper, Shah narrates the case of Arbab Khatoon, who was gang-raped by three men in Sindh province. Shah exclaimed, "She was murdered seven hours later, according to local residents, by her relatives for bringing dishonour to the family by going to the police."

Fake honour killing, technically a perversion of the honour code, is also common. When a woman demands the fruits of her labour from feudal landowners, or asserts her claim to her father's property, she may be smugly killed on a charge of adultery. In the countryside, even the Islamic hereditary law, according to which a female gets half as much from her dead father's property as the male siblings, is not honoured.

Not only this, but other kinds of murders are masked as honour killings, and the practice has become a business of sorts. According to AI, "Reports abound about men who, having murdered a man over issues not connected with honor, kill a woman of their own family as alleged *kari* (adultress) to the murdered man to camouflage the murder as an honor killing." According to Shah, a whole "honour killing industry has sprung up." In one case a man killed his 85-year-old mother on the charge of committing adultery, and then obtained Rs 25,000 (about U.S. $500) from the man participating in the alleged sex act.

There is presently an ongoing debate in Pakistan about changing the name of the practice of honour killings. British colonialists coined this phrase as part of their imperial policy of not interfering with the customs of tribal societies. Asked from where the expression "honour killings" is derived, Nafisa Shah explained, "The practice was common in what is called honour societies, that is, those which adhered to tribal norms and values." Says human-rights activist and journalist Nafisa Hoodhbhoy, "This phrase dignifies the inhuman, decadent practice." Hoodhbhoy added that women's organizations were attempting to devise an alternative phrase to describe the gruesome practice better, "Instead of dignifying it."

Because many of these killings take place in tribal territories— where the writ of the state is almost non-existent—the question has arisen whether the state has any obligation to stop the practice. While the private actors are to be blamed for the abominable practice, Amnesty International says the state cannot be absolved of responsibility. Amnesty points out that Pakistan is party to the Convention on the Elimination of All Forms of Discrimination Against Women (CEDAW), which holds that there must be gender equality under the law. Rejecting the arguments of apologists for the practice, Pakistan's noted educator and rights activist Prof. Anita Ghulam Ali quipped, "Why not? Even in the remotest tribal areas where the writ of the state does not matter, the state can send its representatives to prevail upon the tribal chiefs. They could be explained and made to understand the practice runs counter to human rights and would not be tolerated. If the government showed interest, confidence, commitment, and a political will, the practice can definitely become history."

Sadly, in patriarchal societies, the state may have a vested interest in keeping the dreaded practice alive. Prof. Ali, who is now education minister in Sindh province, explains, "Only those states would have a vested interest, which were keen to see the women were kept in perpetual subjugation." Honour killings are not restricted to Pakistan, where the death toll ranks second after Afghanistan. "It is common all over the southwest Asian landscape: Afghanistan, Pakistan, Iran, Iraq, Turkey, Palestine, Saudi Arabia and right up to Jordan," says AI's local president, Dr Habib Soomro.

In all cases, the dishonour that is brought on a woman does not end with her unsung death. She receives no proper funeral rite. And she is buried not in the common graveyards, but in "cemeteries for the sinners."

IV. Sex Trafficking and Prostitution

Editor's Introduction

Sexual exploitation is one of the most common forms of violence against women. Today the global sex trade is a multi-billion dollar business that effects millions of women and bolsters some of the poorest economies in the world. It is an industry that thrives on increasing economic disparity; women and children from developing countries in Asia, Africa, South America, and Eastern Europe are routinely trafficked to wealthier nations in North America and Western Europe, while men from industrialized countries spend an estimated $1 billion a year on "sex tourism" in places such as Cuba, the Dominican Republic, Nepal, and Thailand. Though many women are driven to this work out of economic desperation, others are tricked into it after accepting jobs as waitresses or nannies abroad; arriving penniless in a foreign land and unable to speak the language, these women are forced to submit to sexual servitude. Other women are kidnapped by trafficking rings or sold into sexual slavery by their own families. In order to break down their resistance, these captives are repeatedly raped and subjected to brutal and dehumanizing torture. Those who manage to escape fear returning home because of the shame their experience will bring to their families.

As Leah Platt notes in her article "Regulating the Global Brothel," Westerners often express sympathy for trafficking victims but look less kindly on women who willingly immigrate to work in the sex trade. She writes that the debate about the morality of sex work—abolitionists view prostitution as a crime against women, while others argue that women have the right to do as they please with their bodies—diverts attention from the abusive and unsafe working conditions in the industry. She argues that sex workers should be entitled to the same protections that are given to laborers in other fields. By legalizing the industry, she writes, governments will be able to regulate it and reduce abuses, such as unhealthy working conditions, assault, and sexual slavery.

Because it is commonly known that prostitutes are unlikely to report an assault, violence is a common hazard for sex workers. In "Long Silent, Oldest Profession Gets Vocal and Organized," Mireya Navarro reports that sex workers in the United States are pressing for greater acceptance and protection under the law. Many hope to eventually decriminalize prostitution, but more urgently, they want to improve their working conditions now. Opponents of decriminalization, some of whom are former prostitutes, argue against legitimizing a practice they believe demeans women.

In "The Link Between Prostitution and Sex Trafficking," a writer for the U.S. Department of State explains why the government opposes the legalization of prostitution. The agency argues that prostitution is inherently dehumanizing and that legalization only increases the demand for human trafficking. Attempts to regulate the sex trade in other countries have failed to address widespread violence and abuse in the industry, the article says. As a result, the U.S. government will not distribute grant money to organizations that support legalized prostitution.

Finally, in "Of Human Bondage," Tara McKelvey reports that a contingent of socially conservative abolitionists have persuaded the adminisration of President George W. Bush to adopt new guidelines for grant applications—guidelines that block funds to any organization that condones prostitution. International aid workers argue that these new restrictions prevent them from distributing condoms to sex workers, placing them at greater risk of contracting the HIV/AIDS virus.

Regulating the Global Brothel

BY LEAH PLATT
THE AMERICAN PROSPECT, JULY 2, 2001

On the night of September 10, 1997, Toronto police officers raided more than a dozen apartments suspected of being houses of ill repute. Twenty-two women, including the alleged madam, Wai Hing "Kitty" Chu, were charged on a total of 750 prostitution and immigration-related charges. All of the women were Asian and spoke no more than a few words of English.

The press accounts of the raid were by turns titillating and full of moral outrage. According to the *San Jose Mercury News*, the women were helpless victims, "pretty, naive country bumpkins" who were exploited by an international crime syndicate (the U.S. police collaborated on parallel raids in San Jose). In a piece for the *Toronto Sun*, with the lurid headline "Sex Slaves: Fodder for Flesh Factories," a reporter profiled "Mary," a Thai prostitute, who obligingly described her first trick, a fumbling failure made to sound almost endearing.

It is a familiar story by now: poor, vulnerable women from Thailand or the Ukraine promised jobs as nannies or models in Western cities, only to find themselves pressed into service as prostitutes to pay off travel debts and line the pockets of their traffickers. As long as the women were portrayed as misled innocents, it was easy for Toronto readers to sympathize.

But readers' pity quickly turned to anger when it was revealed, a few days later, that most of the women had known exactly what kind of work they had been recruited to do. As the *Toronto Star* summed up a few months later, "public opinion did an instant about-face" when police revealed that the women "had willingly come to Canada to ply their trade; wiretaps caught them boasting, long distance, about the money they were earning." Now, the women were considered "hardened delinquents, illegal immigrants, tawdry, dismissible, selling their bodies of their own free will."

Nothing became of the initial allegations of labor abuses. There had been rumors of debt bondage, a form of indentured servitude that requires migrants to finance their travel expenses (which are frequently inflated) by working without pay; of confinement; of shifts that lasted 18 hours. But before these charges could be investigated, the women were released on their own recognizance and disappeared from view, dismissed by the media as common whores.

What is it that separates a Thai woman turning tricks in a cramped Toronto apartment from a Mexican immigrant toiling in a sweatshop in the suburbs of Los Angeles? Why does the former draw our scorn, the latter our sympathy? Clearly, many people react uncomfortably to the idea of sex as just another good that may be purchased on the open market. Yet for the women who make their living as strippers, escorts, prostitutes, and porn stars, sexual activity at the workplace is a job—a repetitive task that can be as unerotic and downright boring as cutting pork shoulders on an assembly line or sewing sneakers in a Nike factory. As such, doesn't sex work deserve the full protection of U.S. labor laws?

One reason that sex work doesn't currently benefit from such labor protections in the United States is that the feminist community, which is the champion of women's rights in the workplace in many realms, remains bitterly divided over prostitution. On one side are the abolitionists, who call prostitution a crime against women, akin to rape or domestic abuse; on the other side are the pro-choicers, for whom the rhetoric of victimization is itself demeaning, and who say that women should be able to do whatever they want with their own bodies, including renting them out for pay.

> *Many people react uncomfortably to the idea of sex as just another good that may be purchased on the open market.*

The two sides talk past each other, particularly at the extremes. Prostitutes, the controversial firebrand Camille Paglia has said, are "very competent, very professional. They look fabulous! I've always felt that prostitutes are in control of the streets, not victims. I admire that—zooming here and there, escaping the police, being shrewd, living by your wits, being street smart." To Donna Hughes, on the other hand, the director of the women's studies program at the University of Rhode Island, the idea of selling a sex act like a trip through the car wash is inherently degrading, and in practice is often accompanied by rape, intimidation, and cruelty. "A lot of people don't know what prostitution is," she told me angrily. "They don't know what it really takes to have sex with five strangers a day. What most people know about prostitution is based on myths and misinformation."

But while feminists debate the "sex" part of sex work—is it degrading or liberating?—they generally ignore the "work" part. Neither Paglia's paean to the hooker-as-rugged-individualist nor Hughes's lament for the little-girl-lost captures the often mundane reality of illicit prostitution: It is a job without overtime pay, health insurance, or sick leave—and usually without recourse against the abuses of one's employer, which can include being required to have sex without a condom and being forced to turn tricks in order to work off crushing debts. Given that the sex industry exists and probably always will (they don't call it the oldest profession for nothing), what should be done about its exploitative conditions?

Sex Work Goes Global

That question was vexing enough when prostitution was primarily a local issue. But sex work is an increasingly global service. In the language of international trade, sexual services are commonly "imported" into places like the United States from the developing world. Men from wealthy countries frequent the semi-regulated sex sectors in Cuba, the Dominican Republic, and Thailand—a phenomenon known as "sex tourism." And women from countries in Southeast Asia, Africa, and eastern Europe migrate to the industrialized world to work in the domestic sex industries. The United Nations estimates annual profits from the trade in sex workers like the Thai women arrested in Canada to be $7 billion.

While there are no precise statistics on the number of women who enter the United States from abroad to work as prostitutes—either voluntarily as immigrants or involuntarily as victims of trafficking—a recent report by the Central Intelligence Agency (CIA) estimates that roughly 50,000 women and children are brought into the country by traffickers each year. (This figure includes trafficking victims who work in brothels as well as those who work in sweatshops and as domestic servants.)

The crime of trafficking in women has recently attracted a great deal of attention from policy makers in Congress and the international community. The European Commission highlighted action against the "modern day slave trade" as part of its commemoration of International Women's Day this March. The U.N. Convention Against Transnational Organized Crime, which was signed in December, included a separate protocol on the prevention of trafficking in women and children.

Here at home, Congress passed the Victims of Trafficking and Violence Prevention Act in a nearly unanimous vote last October, a move that President Bill Clinton hailed as "the most significant step we've ever taken to secure the health and safety of women at home and around the world." Minnesota's liberal Senator Paul Wellstone, one of the bill's co-sponsors, said that "something important is in the air when such a broad coalition of people— including Bill Bennett, Gloria Steinem, Rabbi David Sapperstein, Ann Jordan, and Chuck Colson—work together for the passage of legislation." And what's not to love about a bill that can be dressed up alternatively as a victory for women's rights, a way to get tough on crime, and a curb on immigration? As Ann Jordan of the International Human Rights Law Group puts it, "there is no way that any politician could say he is opposed to this bill. It was a win-win bill for everyone." Even the Christian right was satisfied; Jordan explains that "evangelicals took on trafficking as one of their big projects" in order to rescue innocent women from the sin of prostitution.

But in all this self-congratulatory rhetoric about protecting innocent girls, some of the harder questions never got asked. What is the distinction between "trafficking," say, and alien smuggling, or between trafficking and labor exploitation? According to the CIA report, trafficking "usually involves long-term exploitation for economic gain," whereas alien smuggling is a limited exchange—an illegal immigrant pays a smuggler to be transported or escorted across the border and there the economic relationship ends.

But in practice the two crimes blend together: Hopeful migrants often can't afford the price of their passage and arrive in the country in debt to their smuggler; the smuggler in effect becomes a trafficker. As migrants try to pay off their loans, they are often caught in abusive situations, forced to work long hours in unsafe and unsanitary conditions. The most notorious example of this mistreatment is the El Monte case, named for a town in Southern California where 72 Thai migrants were found in 1995 held against their will

---

The migration of sex workers to the developed world is part of a wider pattern that sociologists call the "feminization" of migration.

---

in a warren of apartments that doubled as a garment factory. To pay off their travel debts, the migrants were stripped of their passports and forced to work at sewing machines for more than 80 hours a week at a negligible wage, surrounded by barbed wire. After the operation was raided by federal and state agents, the perpetrators pleaded guilty to indentured servitude in order to avoid more severe kidnapping charges and were sentenced to between two and seven years in prison.

The facts of the El Monte case parallel the alleged misdeeds in the Toronto brothel: The perpetrator helped immigrants enter the country illegally and the immigrants were forced (either through violence or because of mounting debts) to work in substandard conditions for below-minimum wages. But addressing Toronto-type situations with specific legislation like the Victims of Trafficking and Violence Prevention Act implies that foreign women working in the sex industry are different in kind from foreign laborers in other exploitative industries. There is arguably something to this implication; sex workers are more susceptible to rape and other forms of violent degradation. Yet legislation like the Victims of Trafficking and Violence Prevention Act implicitly seems to exempt sex workers (and their exploiters) from the labor laws that already exist to protect them—making them instead subject to the specific crime of "sex trafficking." Such laws obscure the fact that for the most part the abuses that afflict prostitutes are the sort that can befall all migrant workers.

"Prostitutes," writes Jo Bindman of Anti-Slavery International, "are subjected to abuses which are similar in nature to those experienced by others working in low-status jobs in the informal sector." In her 1997 report, "Redefining Prostitution as Sex Work on the International Agenda," Bindman argues that mistreatment of prostitutes—everything from arbitrary arrest and police brutality to pressure to perform certain sexual acts at work—should not be thought of as hazards of the trade or as conditions that loose women bring upon themselves but as abuses of human rights and labor standards.

In other words, rather than design new legislation to combat the crimes of "sexual slavery" or "trafficking in women," we should prosecute alien smuggling, trafficking, debt bondage, and labor exploitation under existing national and international codes. The International Labor Organization (ILO) has signed conventions on forced labor (1930), holidays with pay (1936), the protection of the right to organize (1948), the protection of wages (1949), and migration for employment (1949), but because of our intuitive sense that sex work should be marginalized as immoral and degrading to women, none of these rules has been applied to the gray market in sexual services. Our well-meaning desire to "protect" women forces the prostitution industry underground and out of the reach of established labor statutes.

Why Prostitutes Migrate

As hard as life can be for prostitutes who lack formal labor protections, it is often still harder for migrant prostitutes, who as both illegal immigrants and participants in an illegal industry are doubly marginalized. The Network of Sex Work Projects, an informal alliance of human rights organizations, warns that the dual "illegality of sex work and migration" allows smugglers and brothel owners to "exert an undue amount of power and control" over foreign sex workers. Employers threaten migrant sex workers with deportation if they inform the authorities about inhumane labor practices—and even if women could report their situation, the authorities might not take it seriously.

The migration of sex workers to the developed world is part of a wider pattern that sociologists call the "feminization" of migration. Until very recently, most labor migrants were men who worked in mining, manufacturing, and construction. If women migrated, they did so under family reunification statutes, often with children in tow. As industrialized economies become more service oriented, the jobs available to migrants are increasingly in the "female" sector, which includes everything from maids to nannies to exotic dancers. "The latest figures from the ILO indicate that more than 50 percent of labor migrants are women," says Marjan Wijers, a fellow at the Netherlands' Clara Wichmann Center for Women and Law in Utrecht. "But the economic situation is different now than it was for men a generation ago. Male migrants entered the formal labor market through formal channels. They didn't have the most attractive types of employment," she notes, "but at least they had work permits. Women have been relegated to the informal sector in traditional women's work: domestic and sexual services, either in the sex industry or in arranged marriages. These jobs are often not recognized as 'work'; there are no labor protections for them, no access to legal working permits."

Despite the very real conditions of abuse, Wijers is careful not to call all low-paid female immigrants—or all migrant prostitutes—victims. For many women now, as has been the case for men for centuries, migration is a calculated financial decision, with prostitution seen as a way to make money. Sex work, like providing paid domestic services and child care, is a way to support family or children back home or to start a new life in the West. "These women made a conscious decision to improve their situation through migration," Wijers explains. "It is possible that they expected another job—and of course, no one expects to be held in slavery-like conditions. But these women are intelligent, enterprising, and courageous. It is quite a step to leave your family and your security to go abroad, into a situation where you don't know exactly what to expect."

Wijers has staked out a defensible middle ground between the strict abolitionists and the prostitution-as-self-expression promoters: She supports a woman's right to control over her own body, as well as a prostitute's volition as an economic actor, without valorizing sex work as a liberating profession. As one of the chief investigators for a report on trafficking prepared for the U.N. Special Rapporteur on Violence Against Women, Wijers is one of the world's foremost experts on forced prostitution, but she finds the narrative of victimization supported by the United Nations to be sentimental and overly simplistic. The reality in her native country, the Netherlands, is more nuanced. "Some of the first women to come from abroad were from the Dominican Republic and Colombia," she says. "They were clearly disadvantaged, recruited in cruel ways, forced into terrible conditions—all the clichés. But when you have spent some period of time in a country, you start to make contacts and to organize. Soon these women were sending for their aunt or their sister—they were organizing the migration of female friends and relatives. Within a few 'generations' of migration, this group of women learned Dutch and became more independent."

One of the most reliable studies of sex tourism, conducted by the ILO in 1998, corroborates Wijers's observations. Based on interviews with thousands of sex workers in Indonesia, Malaysia, the Philippines, and Thailand, the report concluded that "while many current studies highlight the tragic stories of individual prostitutes, especially of women and children deceived or coerced into the practice, many workers entered for pragmatic reasons and with a general sense of awareness of the choice they were making." Almost all of the women surveyed said they knew what kind of work they would be doing before they began; half, in fact, responded that they found their job on a friend's recommendation.

The Benefits of Legalization

In order to use labor laws to protect women in the sex industry, the legal status of prostitution and its offshoots—brothel keeping, pimping, soliciting, paying for sex—would need to be re-examined. After all, the Department of Justice does not ensure minimum wages for drug runners or concern itself with working conditions in the Mob. But whether or not we approve of sex work or would want our daughters to be thus employed, the moral argument for condemnation starts to fall apart when we consider the conditions of abuse suffered by real women working in the industry. Criminalization has been as unsuccessful in dismantling the sex industry as it has been in eliminating the drug trade and preventing back-alley abortions. Sex work is here to stay, and by recognizing it

---

Sex work is here to stay, and by recognizing it as paid labor governments can guarantee fair treatment as well as safe and healthy work environments.

---

as paid labor governments can guarantee fair treatment as well as safe and healthy work environments—including overtime and vacation pay, control over condom use, and the right to collective bargaining.

A decision to re-evaluate the legal status of the sex industry in the United States would not be without international precedent. Prostitution is legal (while subject to varying degrees of regulation) in England, France, and many other parts of Europe. In 1999, Germany eliminated the legal definition of prostitution as an "immoral trade," thus allowing sex workers to participate in the national health insurance plan. Prostitution is also legal in parts of South America and the Caribbean, and in some counties in Nevada. Prostitutes' unions have sprung up in Cambodia, Hong Kong, India, and Mexico, and groups like COYOTE (Call Off Your Old Tired Ethics) advocate for sex workers' rights in the United States.

In areas where prostitution is legal, brothel keeping—or profiting from the proceeds of prostitution—remains a crime. Even the Netherlands, a country notorious for its laissez-faire attitude toward sex work, legalized brothels only in 1999; and the concern that, as sanctioned businesses, brothels would sprout up on every street corner there has proved unfounded. Brothels are now subject to the same building codes and municipal ordinances as any other business—including zoning laws that keep brothels contained in established red-light districts.

As one of the only countries with a fully decriminalized sex industry, the Netherlands provides the fullest illustration of how legalization can operate. Amsterdam's red-light district occupies a maze of narrow streets in the oldest part of the city. Residents who have no interest in frequenting the sex shops can avoid the area without inconvenience. Inside the district, which is marked off with strings of red lights, prostitutes sit in storefront windows to display their wares (100 guilders, or roughly $50, for a 15-minute "suck and fuck"), alongside topless bars, porn and sex toy shops, and the neon lights of peep show emporiums. Even in the dead of winter, packs of foreign men gather in the narrow alleys to gawk and knock on windows. Some of the women behind the windows look Dutch, but Marisha Majoor, who greeted me at the Prostitution Information Center's storefront, corrects this impression. "Most of the blond girls are from other European Union countries, like Sweden and Germany," she says. Dutch women, who can work in the comfort of their own homes, don't bother with the hustle of the red-light neighborhood.

Until last year, Amsterdam's windows were full of illegal immigrants from Africa and eastern Europe. Brothel and club owners estimated that between 40 percent and 75 percent of the women in the red-light district were working illegally. All of that changed with the legalization of brothels. "Of course," says Marieke van Doorninck, a research fellow at the Mr. A. de Graaf Stichting Institute for Prostitution Issues in Amsterdam, "brothel owners were technically never allowed to work with illegal migrants, but the practice was condoned for years. If an illegal worker was discovered, all that could happen is that she would be deported and the club owner would be given a fine. There was no real incentive for the brothel owners to deny jobs to illegal migrants. Now they can lose their license."

There are still a few African women working in the red-light district. Some of them have married Dutch men; others have forged passports from Italy or Greece, allowing them to work in the European Union. One landlord, a gray-haired, heavyset man known as Marcel, owns 20 windows; his "tenants" are mostly from Africa. He claims that all of his "girls" have legitimate papers and, when pressed, pulls out a blue binder stuffed with photocopied passports from Ghana and Nigeria.

The passports may very well be real, but according to van Doorninck, the working papers could not have been. "In other lines of work," she explains, "if a boss can show that there is no person from the EU that can do the job, then he can hire someone from outside." Farmers, for example, regularly request allowances for agricultural workers. "But the sex industry is shut out from this regulation. There is no legal way for a woman from outside the EU to work in prostitution." Sex workers are also specifically excluded from the immigration regulations governing the self-employed. Potential immigrants from outside the European Union "can apply for working papers if they show a viable business plan and can prove that they are capable of taking care of themselves without becoming dependent on the state," says van Doorninck. "But foreigners who apply to settle in the Netherlands as self-employed prostitutes are in principle rejected on the grounds that their activities do not serve the country's interests."

The women working in Marcel's windows are lucky. Most of the Asian, African, and eastern-European women left in Amsterdam are working on the street or in unregulated black-market brothels. "By making it more difficult for foreign women to work in legal places, where they have been condoned for ages, they are forced to leave or to work in an illegal setting," van Doorninck points out. "In a way, the government stimulates trafficking by leaving no options for the women who are already here."

The Dutch government's decision to regulate brothels was based less on morality than on economics. The sex sector had long been "officially tolerated" (or in Dutch, *gedoogt*); by legalizing its activities, the government is able to collect revenues from licenses and taxes. And from the workers' perspective, legalizing the sex industry—and thus barring foreign women from working in licensed brothels—follows from a classic trade-protectionist motive. Why offer jobs to non-Europeans when there are plenty of women in Holland and elsewhere in the European Union who are willing to work in the Dutch sex industry?

Before the change in brothels' status, "there was definitely tension between Dutch prostitutes and the migrant workers, a competition over prices," remembers Wijers. "Because the illegal women had no documents, they were willing to work for less and Dutch women started to feel uneasy." Foreign women "spoil the market," the Prostitution Information Center's Majoor told a team of American and Dutch college students researching the condition of illegal prostitutes last year. "It makes you furious when some guy keeps knocking at your door, saying, 'Okay, but a little way down the street, they are only asking 25 guilders.'" Majoor, like most of the Dutch women who work in the sex industry, belongs to the Red Thread, a lobbying group akin to a union. The Red Thread does not allow illegal migrants to join. "When a hotel like the Hilton suddenly brings in an Hungarian pianist who is willing to work for less money, longer hours, without social insurance, Dutch pianists will complain," Wijers notes. "It is the same mechanism in the sex industry as in other labor sectors."

The Dutch experience with decriminalization suggests that the reaction of the sex industry to the stresses of globalization is not unlike that of, say, the garment industry here in the United States. Domestic workers resent immigrants, who are eager to find work at any pay and consequently create downward pressure on wages.

Arriving in the country with few resources and little command of the language, immigrants are often shunted into the informal economy, which in this case means shady makeshift brothels and back-of-the-bus-station encounters.

Legalization may be limited in what it can do to reach the nearly invisible population of illegal migrants who work internationally in the sex industry. But that's also true of the Victims of Trafficking and Violence Prevention Act and the protocol included in the U.N. Convention Against Transnational Organized Crime. Both of the latter measures define trafficking as an explicitly sexual crime—an act of violence against women—rather than as a by-product of an ever more global marketplace and the increasing feminization of migration. Any policy that will truly improve the often deplorable working conditions in the international sex industry must confront the economic realities of the profession without getting distracted by the sexual ones.

To those who feel their moral hackles rising at the prospect, Ann Jordan of the International Human Rights Law Group presents a compelling analogy: "We don't support a woman's right to choose because we think abortion is a great thing," she says, "but because we believe fundamentally that women should have control over their own reproductive capacity. The same argument can be made for prostitution. Women who decide for whatever reason to sell sex should have the right to control their own body"—and should be assured of basic protection on the job. As with abortions, we can dream of a day when sex work is safe, legal, and rare.

Long Silent, Oldest Profession Gets Vocal and Organized

By Mireya Navarro with Janon Fisher
The New York Times, December 18, 2004

Shelby Aesthetic, a landscaper and writer in Huntsville, Ala., said she worked as a prostitute throughout her teenage years but never knew of a "sex workers movement" until last year, when she caught a performance of a touring art show where prostitutes performed and read short stories and poetry.

"I had done sex work for years and I had never talked to anyone about it," Ms. Aesthetic, 25, said. "I didn't know there was anything out there."

As often happens, a cultural interest opened doors to a social movement, this one involving "sex workers" and their supporters. In a new wave of activism, many prostitutes are organizing, staging public events, and coming out publicly to demand greater acceptance and protection, giving a louder voice to a business that has thrived in silence.

In Huntsville, Ms. Aesthetic—who says that is her real name—recently formed a chapter of the Sex Workers Outreach Project, a California group that itself was created from an organization in Australia last year, and is collecting statistics on prostitution arrests.

At the Center for Sex and Culture in the hip South of Market area in San Francisco, prostitutes meet in support groups, hold fund-raisers, and plot their next political move after having lost a ballot initiative in November that would have eased police enforcement of prostitution laws in Berkeley, Calif.

In New York, they are readying the first issue of a magazine for people in the sex industry for spring publication. And on the Internet, prostitutes have found a way not only to find customers but to find one another. They have formed online communities and have connected with groups in other countries.

Despite the country's conservative climate, the ultimate goal for some in the movement is decriminalization, a move opposed by other former prostitutes who see the business as inherently exploitive and degrading.

For now, though, the activists see ways to push ahead on goals shy of decriminalization, like stopping violence, improving working conditions, learning from foreign efforts to legitimize their work, and taking some of the stigma off their trade.

> *"There are safe ways to work. It's only a risk when it's illegal."*—Carol Leigh, prostitutes' rights advocate

"We call ourselves the rebirth," said Robyn Few, a former prostitute who heads the Sex Workers Outreach Project USA (SWOP) and led the ballot effort in Berkeley, of the current incarnation of the prostitutes' rights movement.

Such a movement has long existed in liberal urban centers like New York and San Francisco, where there is an infirmary for prostitutes named for Margo St. James, the founder in the 1970s of one of the best-known prostitute groups, Coyote (for Call Off Your Old Tired Ethics). But the Internet, coupled with a younger generation of women willing to speak out as current or former prostitutes and tougher federal law enforcement are giving momentum to a more broadly based movement, some of the women said.

Ms. Aesthetic was among organizers of the second national Day of Remembrance yesterday to honor murdered prostitutes. In New York, former and current prostitutes gathered outside Judson Memorial Church on Washington Square Park to read the names of the dead. After each speaker read her segment, the crowd of about 20 people, some holding candles, said "whores' lives are human lives."

Prostitutes and their advocates say the illegal nature of their business makes them a target of violence because a majority of them do not report crimes for fear of being arrested or because they are ignored.

"There are safe ways to work," says Carol Leigh, a longtime advocate for prostitutes' rights. "It's only a risk when it's illegal."

Those who study prostitution say there is a wide range in types, from streetwalkers to high-priced call girls, and in the working conditions they face.

"Some people are doing very well," said Juhu Thukral, a lawyer and director of the Urban Justice Center's Sex Workers Project in New York City, which offers legal representation to the women and researches the field. "Others are really doing it out of desperation."

Advocates of prostitute rights contend that it is a viable source of income for many women and that sexual activity between adults for money should be treated as any other form of legal labor. Ms. Few, 46, who is on probation for conspiring to promote prostitution, and others say their ultimate goal is to remove prostitution altogether from criminal codes, rather than confining it to legal brothels, as in Nevada.

But opposition to that agenda is just as strong among many other prostitutes. Norma Hotaling, a former prostitute and founder of one of the best known groups working to help prostitutes leave sex work, the SAGE Project in San Francisco, said that while giving prostitutes legal rights might help some women "build a business and make money," it would also feed into the worse consequences of commercial sex.

Some of those working to help prostitutes leave their business see allies in those speaking out for sex workers.

Ms. Hotaling said that there was a connection between those who hired prostitutes and those who sexually exploited children and that there was damage to the spirit of women who had no other options for a livelihood.

"It's not just women's rights," she said. "We really haven't talked about what it means to increase the demand and legitimize the buying and selling of human beings."

But some of those working to help prostitutes leave their business see allies in those speaking out for sex workers. Celia Williamson, an assistant professor of social work at the University of Toledo in Ohio, said common ground could be found on calling public attention to the violence and lack of social services faced by streetwalkers, the most vulnerable of prostitutes.

Ms. Williamson says her research shows that most of these women are victims of "sadistic and predatory" violence by customers, and scores suffer from drug addiction and mental illness. Last September, Ms. Williamson organized a conference to help spur a national strategy to deal with the problems.

"Mostly we're sick and tired," said the social worker, who is chairwoman of the advisory board to an outreach program for prostitutes in Toledo. "Prostitution is like domestic violence 20 years ago. Nobody wants to talk about it. Police officers have a lot of discretion. There's no institutional support."

Few people predict that prostitutes are anywhere near obtaining legal rights, but some experts note that there are gains to be had if the movement perseveres.

Ronald Weitzer, a professor of sociology at George Washington University and the author of "Sex for Sale: Prostitution, Pornography and the Sex Industry," said realistic goals included training police officers to respond properly to prostitutes' complaints. The police could also steer resources from revolving-door arrests to referrals to social service programs, he said.

"There's some discretion," Mr. Weitzer said.

In the meantime, some of the women continue their political work. At the St. James Infirmary in San Francisco, Alexandra Lutnick, 26, a research coordinator for the program, said the infirmary not only offered health services but also collected data "to inform policy."

"We can be discounted and ignored as sex workers," said Ms. Lutnick, who has worked in the trade, "but if you go into it as an organization that's seen 500 participants in the last year and 70 percent of them are saying they're being harassed by police, then it's harder to dismiss."

Ms. Few said her ballot measure was just the beginning. "We're not quiet," she said. "We're moving forward. We're not just prostitutes around here."

The Link Between Prostitution and Sex Trafficking

U.S. DEPARTMENT OF STATE, BUREAU OF PUBLIC AFFAIRS, NOVEMBER 24, 2004

The U.S. Government adopted a strong position against legalized prostitution in a December 2002 National Security Presidential Directive based on evidence that prostitution is inherently harmful and dehumanizing, and fuels trafficking in persons, a form of modern-day slavery.

Prostitution and related activities—including pimping and patronizing or maintaining brothels—fuel the growth of modern-day slavery by providing a façade behind which traffickers for sexual exploitation operate.

Where prostitution is legalized or tolerated, there is a greater demand for human trafficking victims and nearly always an increase in the number of women and children trafficked into commercial sex slavery.

Of the estimated 600,000 to 800,000 people trafficked across international borders annually, 80 percent of victims are female, and up to 50 percent are minors. Hundreds of thousands of these women and children are used in prostitution each year.

Women and children want to escape prostitution.

The vast majority of women in prostitution don't want to be there. Few seek it out or choose it, and most are desperate to leave it. A 2003 study first published in the scientific *Journal of Trauma Practice* found that 89 percent of women in prostitution want to escape.[1] And children are also trapped in prostitution—despite the fact that international covenants and protocols impose upon state parties an obligation to criminalize the commercial sexual exploitation of children.

Prostitution is inherently harmful.

Few activities are as brutal and damaging to people as prostitution. Field research in nine countries concluded that 60–75 percent of women in prostitution were raped, 70–95 percent were physically assaulted, and 68 percent met the criteria for post traumatic stress disorder in the same range as treatment-seeking combat veterans[2] and victims of state-organized torture.[3] Beyond this

---

Article from the official Web site of the U.S. Department of State, *www.state.gov*.

shocking abuse, the public health implications of prostitution are devastating and include a myriad of serious and fatal diseases, including HIV/AIDS.

A path-breaking, five-country academic study concluded that research on prostitution has overlooked "[t]he burden of physical injuries and illnesses that women in the sex industry sustain from the violence inflicted on them, or from their significantly higher rates of hepatitis B, higher risks of cervical cancer, fertility complications, and psychological trauma."[4]

State attempts to regulate prostitution by introducing medical check-ups or licenses don't address the core problem: the routine abuse and violence that form the prostitution experience and brutally victimize those caught in its netherworld. Prostitution leaves women and children physically, mentally, emotionally, and spiritually devastated. Recovery takes years, even decades—often, the damage can never be undone.

Prostitution creates a safe haven for criminals.

Legalization of prostitution expands the market for commercial sex, opening markets for criminal enterprises and creating a safe haven for criminals who traffic people into prostitution. Organized crime networks do not register with the government, do not pay taxes, and do not protect prostitutes. Legalization simply makes it easier for them to blend in with a purportedly regulated sex sector and makes it more difficult for prosecutors to identify and punish those who are trafficking people.

The Swedish Government has found that much of the vast profit generated by the global prostitution industry goes into the pockets of human traffickers. The Swedish Government said, "International trafficking in human beings could not flourish but for the existence of local prostitution markets where men are willing and able to buy and sell women and children for sexual exploitation."[5]

To fight human trafficking and promote equality for women, Sweden has aggressively prosecuted customers, pimps, and brothel owners since 1999. As a result, two years after the new policy, there was a 50 percent decrease in women prostituting and a 75 percent decrease in men buying sex. Trafficking for the purposes of sexual exploitation decreased as well.[6] In contrast, where prostitution has been legalized or tolerated, there is an increase in the demand for sex slaves[7] and the number of victimized foreign women—many likely victims of human trafficking.[8]

Grant-making implications of the U.S. government policy.

As a result of the prostitution-trafficking link, the U.S. government concluded that no U.S. grant funds should be awarded to foreign non-governmental organizations that support legal state-regulated prostitution. Prostitution is not the oldest profession, but the oldest form of oppression.

For more information, please log on to the Web site of the State Department's Office to Monitor and Combat Trafficking in Persons at *www.state.gov/g/tip*.

Notes

1. Farley, Melissa, et al. 2003. "Prostitution and Trafficking in Nine Countries: An Update on Violence and Posttraumatic Stress Disorder." *Journal of Trauma Practice*, Vol. 2, No. 3/4: 33–74; and Farley, Melissa. ed. 2003. *Prostitution, Trafficking, and Traumatic Stress*. Haworth Press, New York.

2. Farley, et al.

3. Ramsay, R., et. al. 1993. "Psychiatric Morbidity in Survivors of Organized State Violence Including Torture." *British Journal of Psychiatry*, 162:55–59.

4. Raymond, J., et al. 2002. *A Comparative Study of Women Trafficked in the Migration Process*. Ford Foundation, New York.

5. Swedish Ministry of Industry, Employment, and Communications. 2004. *Fact Sheet: Prostitution and Trafficking in Women*. http://www.sweden.gov.se/content/1/c6/01/87/74/6bc6c972.pdf.

6. Ekberg, G. S. 2001. "Prostitution and Trafficking: The Legal Situation in Sweden." Paper presented at Journées de formation sur la mondialisation de la prostitution et du traffic sexuel. Association québécoise des organismes de coopération internationale. Montréal, Quebec, Canada.

7. Malarek, Victor. *The Natashas: Inside the New Global Sex Trade*. Arcade Publishing, New York, 2004.

8. Hughes, Donna M. 2002. *Foreign Government Complicity in Human Trafficking: A Review of the State Department's 2002 Trafficking in Persons Report*. Testimony before the U.S. House Committee on International Relations. Washington, D.C., June 19, 2002.

Of Human Bondage

By Tara McKelvey
The American Prospect, November 2, 2004

On August 6, Christina Arnold found herself in Svay Pak, Cambodia, an area full of wooden shacks, bars, and brothels 11 kilometers from the capital city of Phnom Penh. Arnold, the 29-year-old director of Project Hope International, a nonprofit organization committed to assisting survivors of human trafficking, had traveled there to visit with social workers, health-care workers, and others who help prostitutes. It's exhausting and grim work; many of the prostitutes are children (as young as 6) servicing Western tourists who hang out at the Home Away from Home café and prowl the area for "small-small," as the young girls are known.

For years, the health-care educators and social workers had worked closely with the children, who are living "by hook or by crook, doing tricks," says Arnold. They tried to teach the girls how to care for themselves. "They would tell the children, 'You will get out of this. There's a way out,'" says Arnold. "'In the meantime, here's how to use a condom.'"

But that was before University of Rhode Island professor Donna Hughes started accusing nongovernmental organizations of teaching children "how to be prostitutes." On April 3, 2003, she testified before the Senate Foreign Relations Committee, saying, "It is unacceptable to provide medical services and condoms to enslaved people and ignore the slavery."

Her words had a chilling effect on health-care workers in Svay Pak. "We were standing on a muddy street, talking to a woman who works for one of these organizations," says Arnold. "We asked, 'So you're not able to deal with children?' 'No, not at all,' she said. 'Unless we want to get shut down.' She looked very upset, and she was holding her face in her hands. The children there are very confused. NGO workers told us pedophiles now know they can go and have unprotected sex with children because the health-education programs have stopped." Arnold paused, then added, "And when children come to the NGO workers and ask for help, they are being turned away."

The woman Arnold spoke with has already lost some funding, and her situation could become even more precarious. Three days before Arnold spoke with her, the U.S. Agency for International Development's Office of Acquisition and Assistance issued new guidelines, which took effect immediately, for international organizations that receive federal funds to fight the trade in human trafficking, a problem that has exploded in the last 10 years. The organizations are not allowed "to promote, support, or advocate for the legalization or practice of prostitution."

> *The problem of human trafficking has existed since, well, forever.*

On its face, this proposition does not sound as if it should be controversial. But the regulatory change has sparked an intense debate within the coalition of groups—left, right, and nonpartisan—that has been working together since 1998 to fight human trafficking. Some, like Arnold, believe the change prevents groups from doing any outreach at all that will help girls trapped in prostitution. Others see the change as a sop to the religious right, which has taken an undoubtedly sincere interest in the problems of trafficking and slavery, but which, to critics, is creating a rift in a coalition that was working smoothly by imposing its value system in a manner that's alienating groups that used to get along—and that isn't necessarily helping the women it's designed to help.

How you feel about prostitution, say program officers, field workers, and human-rights advocates, has become a litmus test for the Bush administration. If you don't have the right views, you're not going to get any money. Or, as one person who works for an NGO describes the new policy, in a phrase that might have a familiar ring to students of the administration's anti-terrorism rhetoric, "You're either with us or you're against us."

Sitting in a corner office at 18th and G Streets in Washington, D.C., John R. Miller, 66, a dapper man in a crisp suit and navy suspenders who is director of the U.S. State Department's Office to Monitor and Combat Trafficking in Persons, waves his hand in the air and swoops in so close when he talks that you can feel his breath on your skin. His office is large and comfortable, filled with chairs upholstered in royal blue, an American flag, and a framed red-and-white Solidarnosc poster given to him by a Polish friend.

"There are plenty of Americans who still say, 'Slavery? Didn't that end with the American Civil War?'" says Miller, a former Republican representative from Washington state, explaining how he has worked hard to raise awareness of human trafficking since he joined the State Department in December 2002.

As he talks, he picks up a glossy edition of the "Trafficking in Persons Report," issued on June 14, and flips through the pages. As the report explains, 600,000 to 800,000 men, women, and children—roughly half under the age of 18, according to estimates—are trafficked each year across national borders. They're forced to work for little or no pay in places like India's brick kilns, Colombia's army barracks, and Cambodia's bordellos.

The problem of human trafficking has existed since, well, forever. But it ballooned in the 1990s after the crumbling of the Soviet Union. At the time, borders became more porous in central Europe, and the trade in humans boomed. These days, human trafficking follows roughly the same routes as weapons and narcotics.

Left unchecked, human trafficking will become the most lucrative of the three criminal industries within 10 years, Deputy Secretary of State Richard Armitage said at a trafficking conference in February 2003. Profits flow to the people who smuggle women across borders and to those who press them into servitude. It can be more lucrative than narcotics: If you're a dealer, you can only sell a bag of cocaine once; if you're a pimp, you can peddle your wares over and over again.

The annual State Department report, which first appeared after the passage of the Trafficking Victims Protection Act of 2000, evaluates how effectively 140 different countries are fighting trafficking, prosecuting criminals, and supporting programs that protect victims. Cuba and North Korea are in "Tier 3," which means the United States may withhold nonhumanitarian assistance until they get their acts together. (The United States is not ranked in this report.)

Besides publishing an expanded edition of the report, Miller has overseen an increase in the percentage of "faith-based" organizations that receive funding (from 7 percent in 2002, according to Caroline Tetschner, a State Department spokeswoman, to 22 percent in 2003); made sure funding is denied to international organizations that do not follow strict guidelines in opposing prostitution; and encouraged changes in the Uniform Code of Military Justice, which will soon forbid military personnel from patronizing prostitutes.

Overall, the Bush administration has devoted more than $295 million in anti-trafficking program assistance in more than 120 countries, according to the State Department. More than 2,800 people around the world have been convicted of trafficking-related crimes in the past three years, and 24 countries have enacted new anti-trafficking legislation. One of George W. Bush's favorite U.S. programs is the International Justice Mission (IJM), which is run by Gary Haugen, 41, author of *Good News About Injustice*, and Sharon Cohn, 34, the organization's vice president of interventions, who has overseen brothel raids in Cambodia.

It's impressive stuff. But human-rights activists, program officers, and health-care educators who work to help trafficking victims describe a dark side to the "abolitionist" movement. The movement's most prominent figures include right-wing policy-makers, a Jewish "moral entrepreneur," and evangelical leaders, whom critics call overzealous and moralistic. Together, the "abolitionists" have formed a potent political force ("It's the most powerful coalition for human rights in America today—perhaps in the world—all under the radar screen of the press," says one of its adherents) known for steamrolling opponents and stifling dissenting voices. Some say they're even snuffing out organizations that don't adhere to a party line regarding prostitution.

Organizations are denied funds if they refuse to sign a "loyalty oath," as one senior officer with an NGO describes a new clause on federal-aid contracts that require grant recipients to say they oppose prostitution.

In addition, Bush's most celebrated programs, including the IJM, are scorned by anti-trafficking activists in places where they operate. A brothel raid led by the IJM last May in Thailand resulted in the freeing of 29 women. But the women were arrested, and to some, it didn't feel much like freedom. "The women became very annoyed when told they had been 'rescued,'" say the authors of a Shan Women's Action Network report. "They said, 'How can you say this is a rescue when we were arrested?'"

And though the particular fates of these 29 women are unclear, experts say it's often the case that when prostitutes—many of whom come from the notorious Shan State in Burma (now officially called Myanmar), where systematic rape and human-rights abuses are common—are "freed" from Thai brothels, they end up in a worse situation. Legally, these women cannot claim refugee status in Thailand. "After 'rescue,' their situation will be made known to Burmese authorities, local village officials and family members," according to the report. "Under these circumstances, a safe and beneficial return home is impossible."

For Cohn, the important thing is freeing women and children from bondage. She speaks convincingly about the horrors of being "serially raped," especially if you're a 6-year-old child. And she's proud of the fact that, so far in 2004, the IJM has saved 152 victims of child sexual exploitation and trafficking. IJM officers try to follow up with the women and children they've saved and make sure they're OK, she says.

Regarding the Thailand episode, Cohn says: "It's probably safe to say we have a different perspective of the raid. Seven underage girls were rescued. If there's even one girl, she'd still have the right not to be raped day and night."

Miller has run into opposition not just from the usual suspects among on-the-ground advocates from NGOs. People within the State, Justice, and other departments have become incensed. Recently, Miller has expanded his reach to the Department of Defense, which will change its military code so soldiers can be court-martialed for visiting a prostitute.

And there have been minor diplomatic dustups. The "Trafficking in Persons Report" contained a case study of a 15-year-old Thai girl taken to Tokyo and raped in a karaoke bar. The report concealed the girl's real name and called her "Sirikit." As it turns out, Sirikit is the name of a venerated Thai queen, and it wasn't pleasant when news of this goof reached the Thai press. "Oh, my gosh, it was terrible," says Miller, nearly climbing out of his chair. "It's embarrassing. We had to send them an apology."

On a more serious level, people who've met Miller and worked with his staff say he's created an atmosphere of fear and intimidation. Some people have suffered recriminations, been "blacklisted," or lost their funds. Yet according to several sources, none of whom was at all willing to speak on the record, Miller isn't even the kingpin.

The muscle guy in the "abolitionist" movement is Michael Horowitz, 66. A Jewish kid from the Bronx who went to City College and then to Yale Law School, Horowitz served as general counsel for the Office of Management and Budget under Ronald Reagan, and is now a senior fellow at the Hudson Institute in Washington. Referred to by author Allen Hertzke as a "moral entrepreneur" in Hertzke's newly published book, *Freeing God's Children*, Horowitz is the one, activists and program officers say, who calls the shots.

The other leading figures are Charles Colson, a former Nixon counsel and an influential evangelical leader; Donna Hughes, the University of Rhode Island professor whose congressional testimony helped lay the groundwork for the August 2004 change in federal contracts and who writes articles on the subject for the *National Review*; Laura Lederer, a former anti-pornography crusader; and Lisa Thompson, a trafficking specialist with the Salvation Army. "Horowitz is the Charlie to their Angels," says an administration official.

Last year, Horowitz, Colson, and others decided to oust Miller's predecessor, Nancy Ely-Raphael. She was an "apparatchik," says Horowitz. "She was just a nice Ferragamo-wearing lady," counters a former Republican staffer on the Hill.

Regardless of Ely-Raphael's taste in shoes, Horowitz, Colson, and other evangelical leaders told the White House to dump her. They wanted to install Miller—even though Karl Rove didn't like him, according to a private e-mail footnoted in the Hertzke book. Rove objected to Miller because he'd supported John McCain in 2000.

In a show of strength, Horowitz and Colson prevailed over Rove, who allowed them to anoint Miller as director of what would soon become the "abolitionist" outpost in the State Department. These days, Miller is in close contact with speechwriter Michael Gerson and others in the White House. "They've told me how concerned he [Bush] is about this issue, and they call me up a lot," says Miller.

And, apparently, they take notes. In Bush's September 23, 2003, speech at the United Nations, says Miller, "he spent 20 percent of his speech" on trafficking. Bush talked about trafficking on the campaign trail on July 16 in Tampa, Florida, and again at the U.N. on September 21. Bush's focus on trafficking is a victory for Horowitz and evangelical leaders in their efforts to influence U.S. foreign policy.

"It's the second act in what is a seven- or eight-act play," says Horowitz.

The dramatic arc of the play, at least according to Horowitz, includes the International Religious Freedom Act of 1998; the Sudan Peace Act of 2002; the North Korea Human Rights Act of 2004, which has been passed by Congress; and an upcoming bill that will alter foreign policy so its main objective will be "the collapse of dictatorship through peaceful means and the promotion of democracy," he explains.

In terms of scope, financial resources, and the president's attention, though, the anti-trafficking initiative may be the "abolitionists'" crowning achievement. The campaign took off in January 1998, when Horowitz began to forge bonds with evangelical leaders like Colson and feminists such as Gloria Steinem and Jessica Neuwirth of Equality Now. They all worked together on a global campaign to fight trafficking and, along with it, prostitution.

"The 'abolitionists' truly believe all prostitution is trafficking, and if a woman says she did enter it voluntarily, she's mistaken. It's the conflating of trafficking and prostitution," says Martina Vandenberg, an attorney with the Washington law firm Jenner & Block and a former Human Rights Watch researcher.

Many people—not only evangelicals and Equality Now feminists—think prostitution should be eradicated. Selling your body is a lousy job. And no amount of "ergonomic mattresses" and "minimum-wage standards," as Horowitz says, are going to make it better. For them, AIDS is an occupational hazard. Eighty percent "suffer violence-related injuries," according to a 2002 study cited in *Violence Against Women.* And in a recent mortality study of 1,600 women in the United States, published in the *American Journal of Epidemiology*, murder accounts for 50 percent of prostitute deaths.

Many people—not only evangelicals and Equality Now feminists—think prostitution should be eradicated.

Partly because of the efforts of the "abolitionists," the Trafficking Victims Protection Reauthorization Act of 2003 stipulates that international organizations receiving funds cannot support prostitution in any way. It's a refined version of the previous bill. The new one includes specific language about prostitution and federal funds. As with most bureaucratic moves, though, the changes took awhile to kick in. This past summer, the official requirements of the act—and the realities of what the Bush administration is trying to achieve—started to appear in contracts required for international organizations that receive federal funds.

Even NGO officials who stop short of complaining about a "loyalty oath" argue that the act hinders their ability to do their work. "Right now, the administration policy is to require foreign organizations to have an explicit policy opposing prostitution," says Cara

Thanassi, senior legislative adviser of CARE USA. "We're concerned it limits our ability to carry out HIV/AIDS and other programs with prostitutes."

Some groups have lost funding. "We fell victim to it," says Layli Miller-Muro, executive director of the Tahirih Justice Center, a Virginia-based organization that, among other activities, provides legal services to trafficking victims. "We were denied a grant to help women in India on that basis. They told us that flat out. I happen to be a religious person. I hold moral views. But it's not relevant to helping victims. The policy against prostitution is a distraction."

The Bush administration has done some good work, raising awareness of the issue and passing new laws, including one—the PRO-TECT Act—that allows U.S. law-enforcement officers to prosecute Americans who've traveled abroad to sexually abuse children. Newly funded programs like the IJM have, literally, saved women and children from hell. But emphasizing victim rescues—and vilifying those who try to work with prostitutes—have unintended consequences. Some of the "liberated" women have suffered in the aftermath. And many anti-trafficking leaders have been shunned because they've refused to sign a contract that supports the Bush administration's position.

"We would like to discourage the U.S. government from using its foreign policy to undermine and curtail freedom of expression," says LaShawn Jefferson, an executive director at Human Rights Watch. "This is being used as a tool of silencing people."

V. Muslim Women and the East-West Divide

Editor's Introduction

Since the terrorist attacks of September 11, 2001, the Western news media has shown increased interest in the Islamic world. Given that many Westerners draw most of their knowledge about Islam from nightly newscasts, which typically present images of Muslim women covered head to toe in burqas and stories about the restrictive laws governing some women in the Middle East, it is not surprising that many in the West see Islam as a religion that is inherently oppressive to women. To some extent these depictions fairly represent the struggles of women who live under particular authoritarian regimes, but the circumstances of women living in the Islamic world are quite diverse—as are the many interpretations of the Qur'an. While many Muslim women would like greater rights allotted to them, they do not define their oppression or liberation in the same terms as most Westerners.

As scholars such as Harvard religious studies professor Leila Ahmed have documented, debates about the role of women in the Islamic world are closely tied to the history of Western intervention. In the 1800s European nations justified their imperial policies in the Middle East in part by pointing to the oppression of Muslim women. Ironically, many imperial administrators, most notably Great Britain's Lord Cromer in Egypt, claimed to be liberating women abroad even as they opposed women's suffrage at home. More recently, the Bush administration cited the liberation of Afghani women—who had suffered the loss of many rights under the Taliban—as a benefit of the invasion of Afghanistan. A recent report by Human Rights Watch indicates, however, that while there has been some improvement for women and girls in Afghanistan since the fall of the Taliban, many of the regional and local warlords that the U.S.–led coalition assisted to power maintain the oppressive practices of their predecessors.

Since the development of the United States' "war on terrorism," pundits and political scientists have suggested that differing opinions about democracy lie at the heart of the East-West divide. But in "It's the *Women*, Stupid," Pippa Norris and Ronald Inglehart argue that the dividing factor is actually the differing attitudes toward women's rights. While the Middle East does lag behind other developing regions—such as sub-Saharan Africa and Latin America—in the development of electoral democracy, recent data indicates that people in the Islamic world consider democracy the best form of government. Surveys also indicate that the widest ideological gulf between Western and Islamic states lies in the equality of women: While Western nations have the most liberal attitudes, Islamic nations have the most traditional.

In "Faith & Freedom" Jay Tolson writes that every victory in advancing women's rights in the Islamic world "seems to come with a disturbing counterpoint." While exploring the setbacks and victories in various nations, he points

111

to Iraq and Afghanistan—both fledgling democracies—as test cases for determining whether Islamic law and theology are compatible with international standards of human rights. Tolson also writes that one development over the past decade has been an emerging confidence among Muslim feminists that Islamic teachings in fact support the case for women's rights.

American Muslim feminists also insist that women's rights are compatible with the teachings of Islam, Rebecca Mead writes in her article "A Woman's Prerogative." These women are not interested in the Western model of feminism and argue that the rights granted to women in the Islamic canon predate feminism by more than a thousand years. Yet even if Muslim women were aware of the rights granted to them under Islam, they would not have the social and economic leverage to insist upon them.

In this chapter's final article, "A Mystery of Misogyny," Barbara Ehrenreich explores the connection between Islamic fundamentalism and misogyny. Many commentators theorize that the rejection of women's rights reflects a rejection of Western modernity, but Ehrenreich points out that fundamentalists have willingly accepted Western technology. She speculates that the massive displacement of male workers due to globalization may be responsible—a phenomenon that has been referred to as a "global masculinity crisis." Ultimately, she suggests that the reader should consider the misogyny of Islam as analogous to the misogyny found in Christian and Jewish fundamentalist groups, none of which the author sees as an ally in the struggle for women's rights.

It's the *Women*, Stupid

By Pippa Norris and Ronald Inglehart
Ms., Spring 2004

In the aftermath of 9/11 and American military intervention in Afghanistan and Iraq, many have characterized the current state of world affairs as a "clash of civilizations." Simplistically, on one side stands the Western world of democratic ideals; on the other, Muslim fundamentalist beliefs.

It is a flawed analysis. In fact, it is the matter of gender equality—women's rights—that stands at the fulcrum of this divide.

In making the "clash of civilizations" analysis, popular commentators commonly cite the thesis of Harvard University professor Samuel Huntington, who wrote in his 1996 book, *The Clash of Civilizations and the Remaking of World Order*: "In the new world . . . the most pervasive, important and dangerous conflicts will not be between social classes . . . but between people belonging to different cultural entities. Tribal wars and ethnic conflicts will occur within civilizations. . . . And the most dangerous cultural conflicts are those along the fault lines between civilizations."

For 45 years, Huntington pointed out, the central fault line in Europe had been the Iron Curtain created by the Soviet Union; now, he suggested, that line had moved east: "[It] is now the line separating peoples of Western Christianity . . . from Muslim and Orthodox peoples."

Huntington's "clash" thesis, has been used to interpret the terrorist attack on the World Trade Center as a reaction by Muslim fundamentalists against Western culture itself. Moreover, his prediction of cultural rifts has been used to explain violent ethnic conflicts in Bosnia-Herzegovina, the Caucuses, Israel/Palestine, and Kashmir. But even if Huntington weren't literally predictive, many fear that the Bush administration has made his forcast self-fulfilling after 9/11 by invading two Muslim countries.

But is Huntington's thesis correct?

According to our analysis of research, no—at least not in the ways he defined the clash of cultures.

For Huntington, the gap between the West and the Muslim East is caused by a lack of shared *political* values, which, combined, create democracy. They include separation of church and state, respect for the rule of law, social pluralism, parliamentary institutions, and the protection of individual rights and civil liberties.

"Individually almost none of these factors was unique to the West," Huntington argued, but "the combination of them was, however, and this is what gave the West its distinctive quality."

We believe he's mistaken: New evidence reveals a surprising consensus that both Muslim and Western societies find democracy to be the best form of government. The cultural fault line that *does* divide the world—and deeply—is the one labeled "gender equality." Muslim nations remain the most traditional societies in the world when it comes to determining the role of women or tolerating divorce and homosexuality. And the gap is widening, because as younger generations in the West become far more liberal on these issues, the Muslim world stands firm against any such change.

Democracy? Yes!

It's easy to see what inspired Huntington's thesis about democracy, given the failure of electoral democracy to take root in most states of the Middle East and North Africa. In 2002 about two-thirds of the 192 countries around the globe were electoral

---

Muslim nations remain the most traditional societies in the world when it comes to determining the role of women or tolerating divorce and homosexuality.

---

democracies, yet only one-quarter of the 47 countries with Muslim majority populations were. And *none* of the core Arabic-speaking societies fell into this category. Although Saudi Arabia has announced that it will hold local elections, the Middle East remains decades behind electoral developments in Latin America, Asia, and much of sub-Saharan Africa.

It's often assumed that Muslim countries are lacking in electoral democracies because their citizens have little desire for democracy. Huntington developed his provocative argument without any systematic evidence of such public opinion, probably, in part, because few representative surveys were available that examined social and political attitudes in both Western and Muslim states.

In recent years, however, surveys have been conducted in several Muslim nations by Gallup and by Pew. Also, the World Values Survey (WVS), which has collected evidence from more than 65 countries since 1981, has added research in the past four years from 13 majority Muslim states (Albania, Algeria, Azerbaijan, Bangladesh, Bosnia-Herzegovina, Egypt, Indonesia, Iran, Jordan, Morocco, Nigeria, Pakistan, and Turkey). Culture *does* matter, as Huntington claimed, in that predominant religious traditions leave an enduring imprint on contemporary values. People living in traditionally Christian nations, as well as in Muslim and Buddhist societies, con-

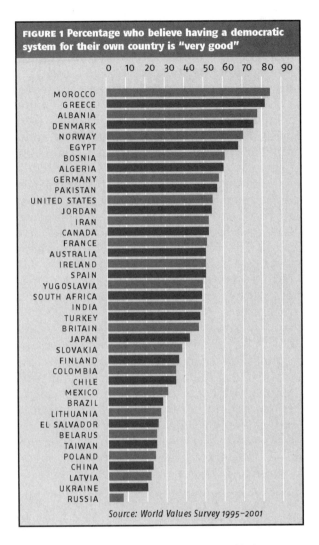

FIGURE 1 Percentage who believe having a democratic system for their own country is "very good"

Source: World Values Survey 1995–2001

tinue to display distinct values from these religious systems even if they've never set foot in a church, temple, or mosque. But that doesn't mean they're anti-democratic.

In fact, the World Values Survey shows that people in Muslim states highly support the statement that having a democratic political system would be "very good" for their country. Indeed, support for that notion in countries such as Morocco, Algeria, and Egypt is far greater than in many established democracies, while attitudes in Jordan and Iran are very similar to those in the United States. The countries most critical of the notion are not Muslim ones but the ex-Soviet states of Eastern Europe, which have experienced radical economic dislocation and a flawed and incomplete transition to electoral democracy.

Support for democracy involves many complex elements, however, and any single survey question may prove unreliable. So we also examined a broader range of social and political topics, including evaluations of democratic performance, since people may believe democracy is the best form of government but remain dissatisfied with the way it works in practice. Still, there is virtually no difference between Muslim and Western publics on these measurements. The country least enthusiastic toward democratic ideals turns out to be Russia, not a Muslim state. Even though it remains unclear exactly what people, given their varied cultural experience, mean when they express approval (or disapproval) for democratic ideals, the loosely defined notion of democracy nonetheless maintains an overwhelmingly positive image throughout the world.

The WVS also includes two items monitoring respondents' attitudes toward the religious leaders in government, and only here are Muslim states in variance with the West: The less-secular Muslim publics prove far more favorable toward active public engagement by religious figures. It would be an exaggeration, though, to claim that this represents a clash only of Western-Muslim values; in fact, the survey shows widespread agreement with the idea of religious leadership in many other parts of the world, including sub-Saharan Africa and Latin America.

Gender Equity? No!

When survey questions turn to gender and sexuality issues, the gap between Western and Muslim publics widens into a gulf.

Support for gender equality was determined by weighing people's attitudes toward women and men in the workforce, education, politics, and the family. The WVS also includes a 10-point scale, ranked from "never justifiable"to "always justifiable," that measures people's approval of homosexuality, abortion, and divorce. It asks respondents to agree or disagree with five statements:

- On the whole, men make better political leaders than women do.
- When jobs are scarce, men should have more right to a job than women.
- A university education is more important for a boy than a girl.
- Do you think that a woman has to have children in order to be fulfilled or is this not necessary?
- If a woman wants to have a child as a single parent but she doesn't want to have a stable relationship with a man, do you approve or disapprove?

The survey results show two striking and significant patterns: First, there is a persistent gap in support for gender equality and sexual liberalization between Western (most liberal), Muslim (most traditional) and all other societies (in the middle). More important, the gap between Western and Muslim publics steadily widens as we move from older to younger birth cohorts. Younger generations in Western societies become progressively more egalitarian than their elders, while younger generations in Muslim societies remain almost as traditional as their parents and grandparents. Moreover,

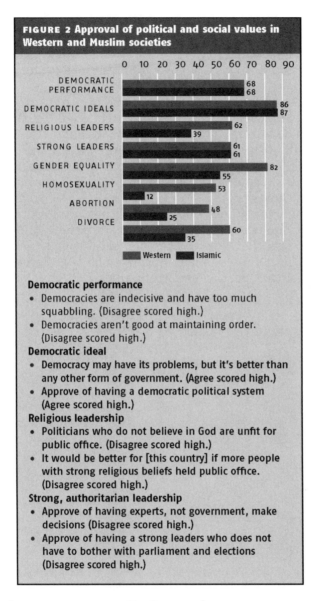

FIGURE 2 Approval of political and social values in Western and Muslim societies

	Western	Islamic
DEMOCRATIC PERFORMANCE	68	68
DEMOCRATIC IDEALS	86	87
RELIGIOUS LEADERS	62	39
STRONG LEADERS	61	61
GENDER EQUALITY	82	55
HOMOSEXUALITY	53	12
ABORTION	48	25
DIVORCE	60	35

■ Western ■ Islamic

Democratic performance
- Democracies are indecisive and have too much squabbling. (Disagree scored high.)
- Democracies aren't good at maintaining order. (Disagree scored high.)

Democratic ideal
- Democracy may have its problems, but it's better than any other form of government. (Agree scored high.)
- Approve of having a democratic political system (Agree scored high.)

Religious leadership
- Politicians who do not believe in God are unfit for public office. (Disagree scored high.)
- It would be better for [this country] if more people with strong religious beliefs held public office. (Disagree scored high.)

Strong, authoritarian leadership
- Approve of having experts, not government, make decisions (Disagree scored high.)
- Approve of having a strong leaders who does not have to bother with parliament and elections (Disagree scored high.)

breaking down survey results by gender, younger *women* prove just as traditional in their attitudes toward sex roles as do younger men.

The differences revealed in the survey results remain significant even after controlling for factors that could potentially affect them, including levels of human and political development, age, gender, education, income, and degree of religiosity.

Policy Implications

The events of 9/11 caused immense interest in the root causes of conflict between the Muslim world and the United States, and Huntington's "clash of civilizations" thesis was but one way of understanding them. Any interpretation, by Huntington or others, carries important policy implications, especially in deciding whether the failure of democracy to take root in many Middle Eastern states reflects the hegemonic grip of governing regimes or deeper currents of public opinion.

But what does it mean when research shows that issues involving gender and sexual liberalization create more Muslim-Western divisiveness than do beliefs about democratic ideals?

For one thing, although vitally important for the process of social change, as well as for progress in human rights, the gender attitude gap is unlikely to prompt international conflict of the sort predicted by the "clash" thesis.

No matter how misguided the U.S. military intervention, analysis of political attitudes in a wide range of comparable Middle Eastern societies suggests that support for democratic ideals does exist in the region. Whether these ideals can ever be translated into stable democratic institutions, however, remains a core challenge.

Faith & Freedom

By Jay Tolson
U.S. News & World Report, November 10, 2003

Muslim women around the world see their future in democracy—and in Islam.

To veil or not to veil is hardly the question. The fate of women's rights throughout the Islamic world today hinges on matters of far greater substance, from reforms of family and penal codes to new understandings of Islamic law and teaching. In these best and worst of times for Muslim women, it is perhaps not surprising that every promising bit of news seems to come with a disturbing counterpoint.

Take Shirin Ebadi, an Iranian lawyer and former judge, who in mid-October won the Nobel Peace Prize for her unceasing efforts to promote women's rights and democracy in her native land.* In response to the jubilant reaction of Iranians throughout the Islamic republic, President Mohammad Khatami—a reformist, no less—dismissed it as "not worth all that fuss!"

Several days after the Nobel was announced, Morocco's King Mohammed VI, who claims descent from the prophet Mohammed, proposed reforms in family law that stand to improve the lot of women throughout the North African kingdom. But long before he presented the reforms to the national parliament, Islamists had taken to the streets to denounce them, dwarfing a pro-reform demonstration by roughly 3 to 1. Also in mid-October, in an unusual instance of Bedouin perestroika, authorities in Saudi Arabia announced that the kingdom would permit the holding of municipal elections within a year—though it's still unclear whether women will be able to run for office or even vote. And at the end of September, in one of a dozen Nigerian states that have adopted *sharia* (Islamic law), a religious appeals court overturned the death sentence of Amina Lawal, 32, a Muslim woman accused of adultery. Yet while Lawal was spared the gruesome fate of death by stoning, at least five other women in Nigeria still face the same sentence.

Women's rights face an uncertain future throughout much of the Islamic world—though nowhere more pointedly than in the constitution-making efforts now underway in both Afghanistan and Iraq. In two nations widely viewed as test cases of the compatibility of Islamic and universal values, it remains to be seen whether and how the principles of *sharia*, or even the more general spirit of

---

* See the appendix for the full text of Shirin Ebadi's Nobel Lecture.

Islamic traditions, will inform their future laws. And behind those uncertainties loom even broader questions facing Muslim women everywhere. In particular, rights activists wonder, are the foundations of Islamic law and theology compatible with international standards of human rights in general and women's right in particular? And if so, what must be done to surmount the practical hurdles—including the crucial matter of who interprets the law—that stand in the way of reconciling Islam with universal principles of women's rights?

Muslim women themselves are already actively engaged with these issues. "When I talk with educated women from Morocco to Pakistan," says Ann Mayer, a professor of legal studies at the University of Pennsylvania's Wharton School and author of *Islam and Human Rights: Tradition and Politics*, "I find that they are much more inclined to evaluate their condition in relation to international standards of human rights. And they say that international standards only reinforce Islamic standards."

Confidence. That underscores one notable development of the past decade: a new confidence among Muslim feminists and human-rights activists that Islamic teachings and sources can support their efforts. This represents a sea change, says Amina Wadud, professor of Islamic studies at Virginia Commonwealth University and author of *Qu'ran and Woman: Rereading the Sacred Text From a Woman's Perspective*. As late as 1995, at the Global Women's Conference in Beijing, many feminists from Islamic countries insisted women's equality could be attained only by jettisoning religion, including the outward trappings of the faith, such as the veil.

Since then, though, an expanding reform movement within Islam, driven largely by increased literacy and an explosion of new media outlets, has led more Muslims to explore the sacred writings on their own. While this has often reinforced the patriarchal viewpoint of militant Islamists, it has also supported progressive and feminist interpretations. Wadud insists that it is unnecessary and even constraining to argue only on the basis of historical precedent, but she finds there is more in the sacred texts and traditions to support notions of gender equality than there is to deny them. She notes, for example, that in the period after Mohammed's death, women, including the Prophet's favorite wife, Aisha, played "key roles in preserving traditions, disseminating knowledge, and challenging authority when it went against their understanding of the Koran or the prophetic legacy."

Referring to the decision of Iran's mullahs to remove Nobel winner Ebadi from her judgeship on religious grounds, Wadud notes, "Nowhere is it said that women cannot interpret the law." Ebadi herself, in a recent interview with Iranian emigre author Amir Taheri, makes the same point in her words of advice to Muslim women: "Don't believe that you are decreed to have an inferior position. Study the Koran carefully, so that the oppressors cannot impress you with citations and interpretations. Don't let individuals masquerading as theologians claim they have a monopoly on understanding Islam."

Fine words, but have they yet had any practical consequences? The answer, many activists say, is a qualified yes. In that widely followed adultery case in Nigeria, for example, Amina Lawal's attorney, Hauwa Ibrahim, got her client exonerated, but on several technicalities that may not work for other women. The real problem, says Mayer, is that Nigeria's version of *sharia* involves a "folkloric version" of Islamic adultery law. First of all, the rules of evidence spelled out in the Koran require either a freely gained confession from the accused or four eyewitnesses to the act of sexual penetration, neither of which was obtained in Nawal's case. Just as important, the maximum punishment for the crime is supposed to be 100 lashes, not stoning.

Illegal. Of course, even if the Nawal case and others did not involve a corrupted use of *sharia*, the punishments that Nawal faced would be in violation of both the spirit and letter of the U.N. Convention on the Elimination of All Forms of Discrimination

Appeals to international agreements have only limited effectiveness in advancing women's rights in the Islamic world.

Against Women (CEDAW), which Nigeria has signed and ratified. But appeals to international agreements have only limited effectiveness in advancing women's rights in the Islamic world. (Saudi Arabia is one of 50 out of the 57 Organization of Islamic Conference nations to sign and ratify CEDAW, but it explicitly stipulates that it will not observe any terms that contradict "norms of Islamic law.") In some cases, appeals might even backfire. According to Wadud, the defense attorneys involved in another Nigerian adultery case had to send out word that any additional international pressure might actually sway the jurists on a religious appeals court not to overturn the verdict.

In a more general way, says New York University law Prof. Noah Feldman, the former U.S. adviser to the Iraqi Governing Council on constitutional matters, the United States faces a similar challenge in its efforts to guide Afghanistan and Iraq toward becoming democratic and rights-respecting regimes. Feldman points out that as long as America is an occupying power, it can accomplish much "just by suggesting"—though, he promptly adds, the U.S.-led Coalition Provisional Authority had to insist on the appointment of several women to the 25-person Governing Council. "But at a certain point," Feldman cautions, "you cross the line to coercing people on how to run their lives."

Feldman prefers to stop short of that line, having disagreed openly with Sen. Sam Brownback and Rep. Frank Wolf's proposal for requiring explicit religious-freedom language in the Iraqi constitution. "Senator Brownback says

> *In Iraq, there are good reasons for thinking that Islam and women's rights can go together.*

if we allow the constitution to mention the word 'Islam,' we'll have problems down the road, but I say if we don't, we'll have troubles immediately," Feldman explains. That does not mean that he has little hope for women's rights. To the contrary, says the author of *After Jihad*, an argument for the future of Islamic democracy, "I am for promoting women's rights by saying they are compatible with Islam."

In Iraq, there are good reasons for thinking that Islam and women's rights can go together. Before the U.S. invasion, says Khaled Abou el Fadl, a visiting professor at Yale Law School, Iraq was one of the most progressive of Muslim nations in relation to women. Not only were there female jurists and lawyers, but there was a civil code that blended the best of French and Islamic laws. Among the latter, he points out, was a law allowing a woman the right to divorce her husband and sue for alimony and child support if he decided to take another wife. (A similar expansion of women's prerogatives is one of the reforms that Morocco's king has just proposed.) Like Feldman, Abou el Fadl worries that attempts to expunge Islam from Iraq's laws will only trigger a stronger urge on the part of many Iraqis to put more of Islam in—and that might mean the most sexist and partriarchal versions of Islam.

Which raises the most important issue: How can Muslim feminists and rights activists win the interpretive struggle against those mullahs and muftis who confuse partriarchal codes and customs with the core principles of the faith? That is a major concern for Irshad Manji, a Canadian author and journalist. Like many other Muslim feminists, she sees the real problem of interpretation as one of overturning Arab traditions of honor that accompanied the spread of Islam and are now being recirculated throughout the world via the Saudi-funded Wahhabi religious establishment.

As Manji explains, within the Arab honor code, individual rights are secondary to one's status within the family or tribe. Women are reduced to "communal or tribal property." In Pakistan or Nigeria, she says, a man from one tribe or family may rape a woman from another as an act of communal retribution. For Manji, who develops her argument in her forthcoming book *The Trouble With Islam*, one of the best solutions lies in women's growing participation in trade, commerce, and capitalism, all of which have been valued since Islam's founding. (Mohammed's first wife, Khadija, was an astute businessperson.) And the economic empowerment of women in the Islamic world is not merely theoretical. It is already underway even in the most Arab of states, Saudi Arabia. In Jidda and Riyadh, respectively, women own a quarter and a third of all businesses. And it is no secret among foreigners working in Saudi Arabia that women are the most educated, able, and productive employees in the kingdom.

By consolidating and advancing their economic position, Manji says, and by becoming tax-paying citizens, women can assert their standing as individuals. This emerging reality is hard to ignore, whether in Saudi Arabia or Iran. Already in Malaysia, Amina Wadud notes, women working through Sisters in Islam and other groups have helped reform domestic violence law by promoting what she calls a "nice blend of *sharia* and civil law."

Still, it is one of the sad ironies of Islam, Manji says, that a religion originally intended to transcend tribalism has, at least in many parts of the world, allowed the tribalist codes to reassert themselves. But Manji refuses to accept that irony as the last word on women's fate within Islam. And she is far from alone.

A Woman's Prerogative

By Rebecca Mead
The New Yorker, January 7, 2002

The women of Afghanistan do not wish to be freed from the stric-
tures of the Taliban only to submit to a Western model of women's
liberation, or so various of their representatives have reminded
well-meaning American feminists during the past several weeks.
"Bring your democracy, not your bikinis" is how Zohra Yusuf Daoud,
Miss Afghanistan of 1973, put it to the audience of a recent conference in New York co-sponsored by Women for Afghan Women. In
fact, there are a number of women in this country whose theological
distaste for the bikini is combined with an appreciation for civil
rights: American Muslim feminists. Some of these women read the
Koran as a document that secures women's rights rather than as a
blueprint for oppression, in spite of the evidence, throughout the
Muslim world, of the originality of such an interpretation. The picture they present of God's plan for women is not quite consistent
with American-style equality; instead, it suggests that the Muslim
woman would be the most pampered, privileged creature on the
planet, if only she knew her due.

Azizah al-Hibri, a Lebanese-American professor of law at the University of Richmond, in Virginia, who is an expert in the prenuptial
contract that traditionally regulates every Muslim marriage, argues
that, according to Islamic jurisprudence based on the Koran, the
contract can be used as an instrument by which a woman can lay
out her expectations about the shape she would like her marriage,
and thus her life, to take. "It goes back to the very early days of
Islam, when it was understood that women entered marriage
equally, unlike previous regimes, in which she was chattel," al-Hibri
says. A woman can secure her right to work outside the home at any
job she likes; she can reassert her right to have her husband support
her financially, even if she has a job or is independently wealthy;
she can keep her finances separate from his and invest them wher-
ever she wishes; she can specify the sum of money she expects to
receive should the marriage end in divorce or should she be wid-
owed; she can negotiate the right to divorce her husband at will,
should he, for example, take another wife; she can reserve the right
not to cook, to clean, or to nurse her own children.

Some American Muslim women even argue that Islam anticipates
the demands of Western feminists by more than a thousand years: a
stay-at-home wife can specify that she expects to receive a regular

stipend, which is not that far from the goals of the Wages for Housework campaign of the 1970s. Elsewhere, the fully empowered Muslim woman sounds like a self-assured, post-feminist type—a woman who draws her inspiration from the example of Sukayna, the brilliant, beautiful great-granddaughter of the Prophet Muhammad, who was married several times, and, at least once, stipulated in writing that her husband was forbidden to disagree with her about anything. All these conditions are based on the canon of Islam and on early Muslim practice, al-Hibri says, but they are rarely applied, since centuries of male-dominated culture have so obscured the essential equality of the sexes at the core of Islamic marriage that a woman's failure to include these provisions in the marriage contract can be understood as implying that she has waived them.

For non-Muslims who fret about the high divorce rate in this country, the concept of a negotiated marital contract that makes explicit the financial, social, and even sexual expectations that

---

The fully empowered Muslim woman . . . draws her inspiration from the example of Sukayna, the brilliant, beautiful great-granddaughter of the Prophet Muhammad.

---

each partner brings to the union has a certain appeal. Although wealthy Americans may have discovered the usefulness of the prenup, the dominant view of marriage in American culture is that it is a largely romantic endeavor rather than an arrangement based, at least in part, on pragmatism. Unfortunately, most Islamic marriages bear about as much relation to this paradigm as most American marriages bear to a Nora Ephron movie. Marriage contracts generally go no further than specifying the size of the bride's *mahr*—a sort of dowry the groom must pay her—because many Muslim women are ill-informed of their rights, and, even if they do know them, lack the financial and social leverage to assert them. Things are even tougher for a woman who might prefer not to marry, or is obliged to remain single. And al-Hibri's pro-woman readings of the Koran are, at times, less than persuasive: in a recent essay for the *Journal of Law & Religion*, she acknowledges that the Koran permits a husband to beat his wife, though she argues that a correct reading of the verse indicates that he should use nothing more injurious than a *miswak*, a twig that commonly serves as a toothbrush in the Arabian peninsula.

A group of Muslim women in Washington, among them Sima Wali, a delegate to the Afghan conference in Bonn last month, has been drawing up a list of legislative recommendations for a reconstructed Afghanistan, including a woman's right to vote and her right of access to medical treatment. Also included is the suggestion that girls receive marriage-contract education in the schools when, as it is hoped, they return to them in the spring. If a particularly bright young Afghan girl should ask why, if Islam is predicated on equality and harmony between the sexes, a woman should be advised to load her contract with conditions that restrict her husband's capacity to exploit her, al-Hibri has an answer. "The way I explain it is that God understands patriarchy, because God created man," she says. "He realized immediately that women need affirmative action." American feminists have never been particularly celebrated for a sense of irony; Afghan feminists, assuredly, will need one.

A Mystery of Misogyny

By Barbara Ehrenreich
The Progressive, December 2001

A feminist can take some dim comfort from the fact that the Taliban's egregious misogyny is finally considered newsworthy. It certainly wasn't high on Washington's agenda in May, for example, when President Bush congratulated the ruling Taliban for banning opium production and handed them a check for $43 million—never mind that their regime accords women a status somewhat below that of livestock.

In the weeks after September 11, however, you could find escaped Afghan women on *Oprah* and longtime anti-Taliban activist Mavis Leno doing the cable talk shows. CNN has shown the documentary *Beneath the Veil,* and even Bush has seen fit to mention the Taliban's hostility to women—although their hospitality to Osama bin Laden is still seen as the far greater crime. Women's rights may play no part in U.S. foreign policy, but we should perhaps be grateful that they have at least been important enough to deploy in the media mobilization for war.

On the analytical front, though, the neglect of Taliban misogyny—and beyond that, Islamic fundamentalist misogyny in general—remains almost total. If the extreme segregation and oppression of women does not stem from the Koran, as non-fundamentalist Muslims insist, if it is, in fact, something new, then why should it have emerged when it did, toward the end of the 20th century? Liberal and leftwing commentators have done a thorough job of explaining why the fundamentalists hate America, but no one has bothered to figure out why they hate women.

And "hate" is the operative verb here. Fundamentalists may claim that the sequestration and covering of women serves to "protect" the weaker, more rape-prone sex. But the protection argument hardly applies to the fundamentalist groups in Pakistan and Kashmir that specialize in throwing acid in the faces of unveiled women. There's a difference between "protection" and a protection racket.

The mystery of fundamentalist misogyny deepens when you consider that the anti-imperialist and anti-colonialist Third World movements of 40 or 50 years ago were, for the most part, at least officially committed to women's rights. Women participated in Mao's Long March; they fought in the Algerian revolution and in the guerrilla armies of Mozambique, Angola, and El Salvador. The ideologies of these movements were inclusive of women and open, theoretically anyway, to the idea of equality. Osama bin Laden is, of course, hardly a suitable heir to the Third World liberation movements of the mid-20th century, but he does purport to speak for the downtrodden and against Western capitalism and militarism. Except that his movement has nothing to offer the most downtrodden sex but the veil and a life lived largely indoors.

Of those commentators who do bother with the subject, most explain the misogyny as part of the fundamentalists' wholesale rejection of "modernity" or "the West." Hollywood culture is filled with images of strong or at least sexually assertive women, hence—the reasoning goes—the Islamic fundamentalist impulse is to respond by reducing women to chattel. The only trouble with this explanation is that the fundamentalists have been otherwise notably selective in their rejection of the "modern." The 19 terrorists of September 11 studied aviation and communicated with each other by e-mail. Osama bin Laden and the Taliban favor Stingers and automatic weapons over scimitars. If you're going to accept Western technology, why throw out something else that has contributed to Western economic success—the participation of women in public life?

Globalization has offered new opportunities for Third World women.

Perhaps—to venture a speculation—the answer lies in the ways that globalization has posed a particular threat to men. Western industry has displaced traditional crafts—female as well as male—and largescale, multinational-controlled agriculture has downgraded the independent farmer to the status of hired hand. From West Africa to Southeast Asia, these trends have resulted in massive male displacement and, frequently, unemployment. At the same time, globalization has offered new opportunities for Third World women—in export-oriented manufacturing, where women are favored for their presumed "nimble fingers," and, more recently, as migrant domestics working in wealthy countries.

These are not, of course, opportunities for brilliant careers, but for extremely low-paid work under frequently abusive conditions. Still, the demand for female labor on the "global assembly line" and in the homes of the affluent has been enough to generate a kind of global gender revolution. While males have lost their traditional status as farmers and breadwinners, women have been entering the market economy and gaining the marginal independence conferred even by a paltry wage.

Add to the economic dislocations engendered by globalization the onslaught of Western cultural imagery, and you have the makings of what sociologist Arlie Hochschild has called a "global masculinity crisis." The man who can no longer make a living, who has to depend on his wife's earnings, can watch Hollywood sexpots on pirated videos and begin to think the world has been turned upside down. This is *Stiffed*—Susan Faludi's 1999 book on the decline of traditional manhood in America—gone global.

Or maybe the global assembly line has played only a minor role in generating Islamic fundamentalist misogyny. After all, the Taliban's home country, Afghanistan, has not been a popular site for multinational manufacturing plants. There, we might look for an explanation involving the exigencies—and mythologies—of war. Afghans have fought each other and the Soviets for much of the last 20 years, and, as Klaus Theweleit wrote in his brilliant 1989 book, *Male Fantasies*, long-term warriors have a tendency to see women as a corrupting and debilitating force. Hence, perhaps, the all-male madrassas in Pakistan, where boys as young as six are trained for jihad, far from the potentially softening influence of mothers and sisters. Or recall terrorist Mohamed Atta's specification, in his will, that no woman handle his corpse or approach his grave.

Then again, it could be a mistake to take Islamic fundamentalism out of the context of other fundamentalisms—Christian and Orthodox Jewish. All three aspire to restore women to the status they occupied—or are believed to have occupied—in certain ancient nomadic Middle Eastern tribes.

Religious fundamentalism in general has been explained as a backlash against the modern, capitalist world, and fundamentalism everywhere is no friend to the female sex. To comprehend the full nature of the threats we face since September 11, we need to figure out why. Assuming women matter, that is.

VI. The Christian Right
and Reproductive Rights

Editor's Introduction

This section continues the theme of the last chapter, examining the conflict between women's rights and traditional religious values. The issue of reproductive rights in the United States has always been contentious, especially for feminists, who see it in terms of a woman's right to bodily autonomy, and religious fundamentalists, who believe that life begins at conception. Most Americans are familiar with *Roe v. Wade*—the 1973 Supreme Court ruling that legalized abortion—but the controversy over reproductive rights actually began in the early 20th century. Margaret Sanger, a midwife and later a social activist, angered religious leaders and faced criminal prosecution for publicly disseminating information about birth control methods. After winning the fight to legalize birth control in 1918, Sanger declared, "Let priests and bishops denounce—let the hierarchy roar! They cannot push the chick back into the shell." Even though the majority of Americans are in favor of family planning, some increasingly vocal religious groups are attempting to roll back reproductive rights to pre-1973—and, in some cases, pre-1918—standards by limiting access to birth control and abortions. The Bush administration has cut funding to the United Nations Population Fund, which works to ensure universal access to family planning, and has reintroduced the Reagan-era "global gag rule," which prohibits international aid organizations that receive funding from the U.S. government from discussing abortion with the women they serve.

In "On Family Planning, U.S. vs. Much of the World," Howard LaFranchi writes that the current White House administration has alienated many in the international community by pressing countries to back down from previously agreed upon family planning goals. Proponents of the administration's position argue that the shift in policy is an attempt to emphasize primary health care over outdated population control policies. Critics of the administration maintain that unmet contraception and family planning needs result in unnecessarily high maternal and infant mortality rates.

In "Christian Soldiers on the March," Jennifer Block argues that a fringe group of Christian fundamentalists are shaping the Bush administration's policies on family planning. Whereas previous administrations typically sent representatives from the American Medical Association and American Public Health Association to international conferences on family planning, the current administration, writes Block, has sent pro-life ideologues. These new delegates have threatened to withdraw aid and stalled on signing treaties in order to push an anti-abortion agenda that many—including some Republicans—deem extreme.

Andrew Sullivan argues in "Life Lesson" that, by framing their arguments in terms of reproductive rights, pro-choice Americans—particularly those in the Democratic Party—have alienated people of faith. While he agrees that abortion should remain legal, he believes that the pro-choice movement would do better to push aggressively for family planning to prevent unwanted pregnancies in the first place.

In the final article of this collection, "Pharmacists Balk on After-sex Pill and Widen Fight," Pam Belluck reports on the growing number of pharmacists in the United States who refuse to fill prescriptions for contraceptives or the morning-after pill because of their religious views. Some state legislatures have passed laws that protect these pharmacists. While the American Pharmacists Association allows druggists to refuse filling such prescriptions, it requires that they transfer the prescription elsewhere to be filled—and in some cases the pharmacists have refused to do so.

On Family Planning, U.S. vs. Much of the World

By Howard LaFranchi
The Christian Science Monitor, March 30, 2004

The world's rising disapproval of U.S. foreign policy stems in part from opposition to the war in Iraq and the "with us or against us" tone of the world's only superpower.

But beneath the focus on geopolitics, such hot-button social issues as family planning and women's reproductive rights are also demonstrating America's shifting stature in the world—especially as the Bush administration seeks to placate its socially conservative base.

In a series of regional meetings on population and development, the U.S. has pressed other countries to back down from goals in family planning and women's reproductive rights, targets set in tandem with development plans and adopted with strong U.S. support a decade ago. At the most recent meeting in Santiago, Chile, earlier this month, 40 countries rejected a U.S. move to stress abstinence over contraception in a declaration, and thus bring it more in line with Bush administration priorities.

U.S. proponents of the administration's redirection of international family policy say the U.S. is simply running up against foreign elites bent on the status quo. Those elites, they insist, do not reflect the interests of developing countries.

But critics emphasize contrary evidence in lopsided votes against the United States at international progress-report meetings.

"It's one of the most drastic examples of U.S. isolation," says Sharon Camp, president of the Alan Guttmacher Institute, an international reproductive-rights organization. Pointing to the Santiago meeting, she adds, "When every country, and in such a Catholic-dominated region, votes against your position, that's a remarkable defeat."

America's solitary stance on reproductive rights and international aid for family planning joins other factors in U.S. isolation—among them, withdrawal from the Kyoto Protocol and rejection of an International Criminal Court.

But proponents of administration policy say the apparent isolation is due to the U.S. emphasis on primary health care over an outdated focus on population control. If the U.S. is isolated, they say, that isolation is only from a global family-planning community the U.S. itself has built up over the past four decades.

"I don't see the U.S. as isolated, I see it as prescient," says Steven Mosher, president of the Population Research Institute (PRI), a Virginia-based organization that monitors population-control abuses worldwide. "The U.S. was in the vanguard back in the 1960s when the focus was the population bomb, and it is leading the way again as the focus shifts from population control to primary healthcare."

As for the 40–1 vote against the U.S. in Santiago and rejections of U.S. positions in other regional meetings, Mr. Mosher says, "The 40 [votes] represent non-governmental groups that have been nurtured by the U.S. in the past and still get funding from the U.N. Population Fund. I can see that it must seem strange to them that the U.S. is now saying we've gone too far down the population-control road."

The debate over international family-planning assistance has become part of a tug of war on women's rights in developing countries.

Under this administration, the United States has cut off funding to the U.N. Population Fund (UNFPA), citing claims that the agency condones forced abortions and sterilizations in China. A team sent to China by the White House in 2002 found "no evidence" of UNFPA knowledge of or support for such measures, but the funding was still halted.

More broadly, the debate over international family-planning assistance has become part of a tug of war on women's rights in developing countries. One side says international policy is suppressing the yearnings of motherhood, at a time when population growth has slowed. The other side says unmet contraception and family-planning needs keep maternal and infant mortality unnecessarily high.

Congressional supporters of the Bush stance on family-planning aid have called the UNFPA and the "consensus" of the 1994 Cairo meeting "anti-woman" and "Taliban-like" for their emphasis on reducing unplanned pregnancies.

But in a recent report, the Guttmacher Institute said developing countries' "unmet [contraception] need"—deduced from the number of women using "traditional methods" or no contraception at all—translates to 52 million unwanted pregnancies each year, bringing on 1.5 million maternal deaths and more than 500,000 motherless children.

"We also estimate that about one-third of [unwanted pregnancies] result in abortion, and about half of those in unsafe abortion," says Ms. Camp. The fact that developing countries cover 75 percent of their own family-planning costs suggests that reproductive policies are a priority, the Guttmacher Institute says.

Critics of the Bush administration's new emphasis of marital fidelity and de-emphasis of condoms say those policies ignore the fact that the fastest-rising segment of HIV-AIDS victims in parts of Africa are young women prized as brides for older men. Others point to what they see as the irony of White House emphasis on its international record of advancing women's rights—primarily through the liberation of women in Afghanistan and Iraq—when so many women's organizations around the world oppose U.S. policy.

But perhaps the bigger irony is that proponents of both sides say the No. 1 priority for women in developing countries should be basic healthcare. "I hope that five years down the road we're taking all the money [for family planning] and putting it into women's primary healthcare," says PRI's Mr. Mosher.

Yet as even proponents of the U.S. position admit, that won't be easy if the U.S. loses credibility on reproductive issues.

Christian Soldiers on the March

BY JENNIFER BLOCK
THE NATION, FEBRUARY 3, 2003

In Jerry Jenkins and Tim LaHaye's bestselling *Left Behind* series (think of it as a Star Wars Trilogy for the religious right—it has sold 35 million copies), one-quarter of the world's population has mysteriously disappeared, and the most God-fearing among those "left behind" form the Tribulation Force, a troupe of evangelicals who believe the End of Days is nigh and the Secretary General of the United Nations is the Antichrist.

There's no evidence that George W. Bush owns the leather-bound collector's edition, but he certainly would sympathize with the T-Force's distaste for multilateralism. To every U.N. meeting that has occurred since he assumed the presidency, Bush has sent pit-bull delegations seemingly bent on ravaging both the global spirit as well as hard-fought consensus built throughout the past decade on social justice and human rights, especially women's rights.

To represent this country to the world, Bush has replaced career diplomats with career ideologues: John Klink, a former chief negotiator for the Vatican, has been on nearly every U.S. delegation to a U.N. meeting, joined by Jeanne Head of the National Right to Life Committee, Janice Crouse of Concerned Women for America—the group founded by Tim LaHaye's wife, Beverly—and others from the "pro-family" lobby.

The Administration's international policies on sexual and reproductive health and rights, meanwhile, have been a Christian fundamentalist's dream. Within hours of the inaugural ball Bush was at his desk reviving the "global gag rule," which essentially corners humanitarian organizations worldwide into hushing up about abortion. He then stripped the U.N. Population Fund (UNFPA) of 12.5 percent of its budget, withheld $3 million from the World Health Organization's Human Reproduction Program, and is now earmarking $33 million—almost exactly the amount he took away from the UNFPA—to augment domestic abstinence-until-marriage "sex-ed." He dispatched his emissaries to throw colossal tantrums at the U.N. General Assembly Special Session on Children, the World Summit on Sustainable Development, and, most recently, the Fifth Asian and Pacific Population Conference, bringing all three negotiations to a near-halt over objections to no-brainer public health concepts like "consistent condom use" for HIV prevention and "safe abortion" where it is legal.

Charlotte Bunch, director of the Center for Women's Global Leadership, sees this attack as part of a larger assault on internationalism in general. "Their overall goal has always been to weaken the United Nations, in particular its capacity to be a constraining force on the flow of global capital and militarism," she says. "Attacking reproductive rights is convenient because it also delivers for the right wing." And it's low risk. "The Bush Administration has been able to get away with what would be appalling to most moderate Republicans," explains Jennifer Butler, the Presbyterian Church's U.N. representative, who tracks the Christian right's activities at the U.N., Very few people—including members of the press—pay attention to U.N. meetings, she observes. "Bush can throw a bone to the Christian right and score some points, and he can do that without a cost."

> *"Attacking reproductive rights is convenient because it also delivers for the right wing."*—Charlotte Bunch, director of the Center for Women's Global Leadership

Bush's first major foray into U.N. politics was in March 2001, when—perhaps still a little high from the fund-slashing frenzy—he sent the U.S. delegation swaggering into the U.N. Commission on Human Rights like "cowboys," according to Bunch. The Geneva meeting is six weeks long, and "one of the most highly orchestrated; second only to the General Assembly in attention to detail of diplomacy," she says. The delegation's behavior was so indecorous that at the end of the session, the Europeans declined to re-elect the United States to the commission for the first time ever (they were invited back after 9/11).

Two months later, Bush sent professional right-to-lifer Jeanne Head to represent our country's global health interests at the annual World Health Assembly, quietly laying off the usual crew of reps from groups like the American Medical Association and American Public Health Association.

The Administration finally attracted widespread outrage when at the U.N. Special Session on Children, held in New York in May 2002, the Tommy Thompson–led U.S. delegation made a grimly ironic alliance with Iran, Syria, Libya, Sudan, and Iraq in the midst of Bush's "with us or against us" declaration of war on Islamic fundamentalists. Together, joined by the Vatican, these culture warriors fought to purge the world of comprehensive sex education for adolescents, restrict STD-prevention and contraceptive information to heterosexual married couples, and redefine "reproductive health services" to exclude legal abortion.

Most of the 3,000 activists and diplomats in attendance came to New York intending to negotiate broader definitions and commit more services to young people, who are becoming infected with HIV at the rate of five per minute, according to the U.N. Instead, they had to fight tooth and nail just to hang on to language already on the books. "The United States really hijacked the whole session," says Françoise Girard of the International Women's Health Coalition. Example: During discussion of a section referring to children in postconflict situations, Washington harped on the word "services" because it might imply emergency contraception or abortion. "Nobody could understand why the United States would oppose language that was basically saying, 'When there are children who have been victims of violence and trauma in war, we need to provide them with services,'" says Zonny Woods of Action Canada for Population and Development. "But because among those victims of violence there might be girls who were victims of rape, who might be offered emergency contraception or an abortion, they were willing to throw away the whole concept of 'services.' It was just insane."

For the global women's movement, the ICPD is considered a watershed event.

The U.S. delegation succeeded in watering down the agreement, removing a paragraph on adolescent sexuality education and also some references to reproductive health services. And it blocked consensus on opposing capital punishment for adolescents, a detail that got lost in the media focus on the U.S. obsession with abortion and abstinence.

At the World Summit on Sustainable Development, in Johannesburg last September, it was, as they say, déjà vu all over again. The United States, again in the dugout with the Holy See and a number of Islamic countries, deadlocked negotiations until the eleventh hour, opposing a litany of items, including language that would characterize female genital mutilation, forced child marriage, and honor killings as human rights violations. "In the end, at 1 in the morning, they agreed to language that was almost identical to what they'd been fighting the whole time," says June Zeitlin, executive director of the Women's Environment and Development Organization. "We got what we wanted. But the United States succeeded in stalling the conference and in alienating a lot of countries."

Then came the real weapon of mass destruction, as far as women's rights are concerned: On November 1, Bush announced that the United States was considering withdrawing its support from the landmark agreement reached by 179 countries at the 1994 International Conference on Population and Development in Cairo. For the global women's movement, the ICPD is considered a watershed event—the first time an official connection was made between population control and empowering women with information and contraception. With the Fifth Asian and Pacific Population Conference in Bangkok looming in December—a regional meeting for delegates to review the advances made in implementing the ICPD, not to revisit its basic principles—the United States was threatening to oppose the document unless all references to "reproductive health services" and "reproductive rights" were deleted.

But this time the Administration miscalculated. "They really overplayed their hand," says Françoise Girard. At an especially revealing moment during the December 11–17 showdown in Bangkok, U.S. adviser Elaine Jones, an international relations officer in the State Department, took the microphone to express her country's—our country's—insistence that natural family-planning methods be emphasized in the conference document, offering her own experience with the Billings method of birth control (which involves checking the viscosity of one's own cervical mucus): "I've used the Billings method for 10 years," Jones announced, "and it works." As titters spread across the room, one of the first of many responses came from, of all places, Iran. "Well, I'm an Ob-Gyn," said the Iranian delegate. "I have to tell you that natural family-planning methods have a very high failure rate. And by the way, it says so in all the textbooks that come from United States."

Less touchy-feely were the threats reportedly made by the United States to individual countries, specifically to the Philippines, Sri Lanka, and Nepal, to withhold their piece of the USAID pie if they didn't vote along with the U.S. delegation. "They were trying to push some governments around pretty hard," said one U.N. official on condition of anonymity.

"This is the fringe who've taken over U.S. policy on sexual and reproductive health," says Girard. "Some people asked me, 'Do you think they're doing this because they want to save our souls?'" One first-time attendee from the United States said, "If they didn't have so much power I'd feel sorry for them."

In the end, however, the U.S. delegation lost everything. When they demanded a roll-call vote on two sections of the ICPD agreement (dealing with reproductive rights and adolescent health) which they found objectionable, the votes came in at 31 to 1 and 32 to 1, with two countries abstaining—notably, Nepal and Sri Lanka. "They thought calling a vote would intimidate the Asians," says Girard, "when all it did was put on the record that the United States was completely isolated." Another observer remarked that the Americans "played themselves out of the game."

Ultimately, the Americans backed down on their threats to renounce the whole agreement, but they stunned other delegations with their "general reservation" to the document, a schizophrenic two-page addendum expressing disappointment that "the promotion of women's full enjoyment of all human rights is not emphasized more often," while also declaring, "Because the United States supports innocent life from conception to natural death, the United

States does not support, promote, or endorse abortions, abortion-related services or the use of abortifacients." (Girard points out that if life begins at conception, the garden-variety Pill would be illegal.) The United States also opposed the term "unsafe abortion," a position explained by Jeanne Head during a 15-minute tirade at the closing ceremony: Abortion is never safe, because someone—the fetus—always dies. Thus the U.S. delegation stated in its reservation, "The illegality of abortion cannot be construed as making it unsafe."

Says Girard, "If there was any doubt that Bush wants to overturn *Roe v. Wade*, it is clear now."

Sally Ethelston, vice president of Communications for Population Action International (PAI), remembers Cairo. "I'll never forget the faces of country delegates the afternoon they had finished their hardest negotiations. People emerged beaming because they knew they had forged something that would take the discussion so much further. And the United States played a major role in that process. What we see now is the United States playing the role of the bully."

"It's like Bush is sacrificing the women of the world to pay his political dues," says Terri Bartlett, also of PAI.

Regardless of whether Bush's machinations are payback to the religious right or born of a core belief that the U.N. will bring about the fall of man, activists in the global women's movement are not taking any more chances. Though many were expecting a 5th World Conference on Women to take place in Helsinki in 2005 (especially the Finns), the present consensus is that a 10-year follow-up to the 1995 conference in Beijing would be far too much of a risk. "Beijing is an incredible document," says Françoise Girard. "You look at it and really say, 'Wow.'" Still, women's activists are quick to insist that Bush isn't the only factor. "I wouldn't give him all the credit," says Zonny Woods. Conferences are a huge drain on time and resources, taking the best and brightest away from their work implementing the agreement. "If you think about it, we've been either having a major U.N. conference or preparing one for the past 12 years."

Indeed, the 1990s were not just about globalization of capital: There was the Rio conference in 1992, then a series of negotiations on climate change, forests, and biodiversity. There were conferences on habitat, population and development, women, social development, human rights; then each of those had five-year reviews; then there were the conferences on racism, aging, and HIV/AIDS; then the Special Session on Children.

"We don't need another conference in 2005," says Charlotte Bunch. "We need to keep working on implementing the Beijing platform. It hasn't been realized. Perhaps in 2010, or 2008, it will be a better political moment."

On the other hand, notes Jennifer Butler, the destructive role of the Bush Administration deserves wide attention. "If we don't tell people what's really going on, how can we mobilize them?" The U.N.

shapes global norms, she argues, and if the superpower breaks away, it gives every other country license to back away from its commitments. "Since Beijing, you can't speak of any major world issue without applying some sort of gender lens," she says. Health ministries have implemented new programs, budgets have been allocated, national policy has been revised. But if Bush is allowed to continue his attack, "we will see a rollback, a slow erosion of the world culture that has been redefined to say it's not OK to violate women's rights."

And it's not only feminists who are fearful. There's plenty of buzz within the U.N. about how these conferences need to be made more, let's say, childproof. "We have got to figure out a way to avoid this again, because this is not productive at all. Because AIDS won't wait. Unwanted pregnancies won't wait," says a U.N. official.

Says Butler, "Maybe it's time to sound the alarm bells."

Life Lesson

By ANDREW SULLIVAN
THE NEW REPUBLIC, FEBRUARY 7, 2005

Hillary Rodham Clinton is absolutely right. I've waited many years to write that sentence, but, hey, if you live long enough. . . . I'm referring to her superb speech earlier this week on the politics and morality of abortion. There were two very simple premises to Clinton's argument: a) the right to legal abortion should remain, and b) abortion is always and everywhere a moral tragedy. It seems to me that if we are to reduce abortions to an absolute minimum (and who, exactly, opposes that objective?), then Clinton's formula is the most practical. Her key sentences: "We can all recognize that abortion in many ways represents a sad, even tragic choice to many, many women. . . . The fact is that the best way to reduce the number of abortions is to reduce the number of unwanted pregnancies in the first place."

Echoing her husband's inspired notion that abortion should be "safe, legal, and rare," the senator from New York seemed to give new emphasis to that last word: "rare." Hers is, in that respect, a broadly pro-life position. Not in an absolutist, logically impeccable fashion—which would require abolishing all forms of legal abortion immediately—but in a pragmatic, moral sense. In a free society, the ability of a woman to control what happens to her own body will always and should always be weighed in the balance against the right of an unborn child to life itself. And, if she and the Democrats can move the debate away from the question of abortion's legality toward abortion's immorality, then they stand a chance of winning that debate in the coming years.

For too long, supporters of abortion rights have foolishly and callously trivialized the moral dimensions of the act of ending human life in the womb. They have insisted that no profound moral cost is involved. They remain seemingly impassive in the face of the horrors of partial-birth abortion. They talk in the abstract language of "reproductive rights" and of a "war against women." To acknowledge that human life is valuable from conception to death has been, at times, beyond their capacity. They have seemed blind to the fact that, as Naomi Wolf once alluded in this magazine, mothers and children have souls and that, in every abortion, one soul is destroyed and another wounded. And they seem far too dismissive of the fact that the concerns of many pro-life Americans are not rooted in intolerance but in the oldest liberal traditions of the protection of the weak.

All this has undermined the pro-choice movement. Its members seem godless in a faithful culture. They have come to seem indifferent to pain, almost glib in the face of human tragedy. Of course, this may not be true in the hearts and minds of many pro-choice activists. But, in the arena of public debate, it is the cold corner into which their rhetoric has condemned them.

How to change? Clinton's approach is the right one. Acknowledge up front the pain of abortion and its moral gravity. Defend its legality only as a terrible compromise necessary for the reduction of abortions in general, for the rights of women to control their own wombs, and for the avoidance of unsafe, amateur abortions. And then move to arenas where liberals need have no qualms: aggressive use of contraception and family planning, expansion and encouragement of adoption, and a rhetorical embrace of the "culture of life." One reason that John Kerry had such a hard time reaching people who have moral qualms about abortion was his record and rhetoric: a relentless defense of abortion rights—even for third-trimester unborn children—with no emphasis on the moral costs of such a callous disregard of human dignity. You cannot have such a record and then hope to convince others that you care about the sanctity of life.

The [Democratic] party needs to end its near fatwa on pro-life politicians and spokespeople.

Clinton did one other thing as well. She paid respect to her opponents. She acknowledged the genuine religious convictions of those who oppose all abortion. She recognized how communities of faith have often been the most successful in persuading young women to refrain from teenage sex. She challenged her pro-choice audience by pointing out that "seven percent of American women who do not use contraception account for 53 percent of all unintended pregnancies." She also cited research estimating that 15,000 abortions per year are by women who have been sexually assaulted—one of several reasons, she said, that morning-after emergency contraception should be made available over the counter. By focusing on contraception, she appeals to all those who oppose abortion but who do not follow the abstinence-only movement's rigid restrictions on the surest way to prevent them.

But even this is not enough for the Democrats to move the issue out of its current impasse. The party needs to end its near fatwa on pro-life politicians and spokespeople. Harry Reid and Tim Roemer are a start. The Democrats should learn from President Bush's canny use of the issue. He is firmly pro-life. And yet he gave several pro-choice politicians key slots at the Republican convention. The new number-two at the Republican National Committee, Jo Ann Davidson, is pro-choice. When the Republicans are more obviously tolerant of dissent than Democrats, something has gone awry. One obvious option: Find every way to back Pennsylvania's Robert Casey Jr. in his campaign to wrest a Senate seat from the most extreme and intolerant pro-life absolutist, Rick Santorum. Or take a leaf from Tony Blair's book. In his cabinet, the 36-year-old Education secretary, Ruth Kelly, is adamantly pro-life as a matter of conscience and is even a member of the ultra-conservative Catholic group Opus Dei. Her personal views on this do not impact her political position—or Blair's own support for abortion rights. But her inclusion in the Labour Party shows a recognition that, on such profound moral issues, party lines are inappropriate—and often self-defeating.

In some ways, this does not mean a change of principle. Democrats can still be, and almost certainly should be, for the right to legal abortion. But, instead of beginning their conversation with that right, they should start by acknowledging a wrong. Abortion is always wrong. How can we keep it legal while doing all we can to reduce its damage? Call it a pro-life pro-choice position. And argue for it with moral passion. If you want to win a "values" debate, it helps to advance what Democrats value. And one of those obvious values is the fewer abortions the better. Beyond the polarizing rhetoric, a simple message: saving one precious life at a time.

Pharmacies Balk on After-sex Pill and Widen Fight

By Monica Davey and Pam Belluck
The New York Times, April 19, 2005

As a fourth-generation pharmacist whose drugstore still sits on the courthouse square of his conservative small town downstate [in Illinois], State Senator Frank Watson knew exactly what side to take when Gov. Rod R. Blagojevich ordered pharmacies to fill prescriptions for women wanting the new "morning after" pill, even if it meant putting aside their employees' personal views.

"The governor is trying to make a decision that must be left to the pharmacy," said Senator Watson, whose family business, Watson's Drug Store in Greenville, Ill., does not stock the pill. "It's an infringement on a business decision and also on the pharmacist's right of conscience."

Senator Watson, the Republican leader of the Senate, and Governor Blagojevich, a Democrat, are the latest combatants in a growing battle over emergency contraception. In at least 23 states, legislators and other elected officials have passed laws or are considering measures in a debate that has attracted many of the same advocates and prompted much of the same intensity as the fight over abortion.

In some states, legislators are pushing laws that would explicitly grant pharmacists the right to refuse to dispense drugs related to contraception or abortion on moral grounds. Others want to require pharmacies to fill any legal prescription for birth control, much like Governor Blagojevich's emergency rule in Illinois, which requires pharmacies that stock the morning-after pill to dispense it without delay. And in some states, there are proposals or newly enacted laws to make the morning-after pill more accessible, by requiring hospitals to offer it to rape victims or allowing certain pharmacists to sell it without a prescription.

Some of the bills could become moot if the Food and Drug Administration approves the morning-after pill for over-the-counter sale by pharmacists, something advocates for women's reproductive rights and several Democratic senators have pressured the agency to do.

If over-the-counter sales are allowed, experts on the issue say, pharmacists who do not want to provide the pill on moral grounds could simply decide not to stock it, which current state laws already allow them to do. If a large drugstore chain decided to stock it, but an individual pharmacist in the chain objected, such a dispute might be governed by the employment agreements between the chain and the pharmacist.

But the bills may also lay the groundwork for pharmacists' actions regarding future controversial medications. And both sides in the debate may consider the publicity generated by any proposed legislation to be beneficial to their cause.

"This is going to be a huge national issue in the future," said Paul Caprio, director of Family-Pac, a conservative group that urged pharmacists in Illinois to ignore Governor Blagojevich's rule. "Pharmacists are coming forward saying that they want to exercise their rights of conscience."

Nancy Keenan, the president of Naral Pro-Choice America, said she believed the issue was blocking women in many parts of the country from getting morning-after prescriptions filled, though she had no firm statistics. "It's difficult to get the hard numbers because there's not a mechanism for women to report this," she said. "But we have heard about cases from Beverly Hills to Wisconsin, Massachusetts, Chicago—it seems to be all over the country."

In Illinois, Governor Blagojevich enacted his emergency rule after hearing of two women who said a pharmacist had refused to fill their morning-after pill prescriptions at a drugstore downtown this year. Penalties against a pharmacy can range from a fine to revocation of its license to dispense drugs.

Since April 1, officials at the governor's office say, two more people have filed complaints to an emergency hot line about similar situations. On Monday, Governor Blagojevich submitted paperwork to try to make his emergency rule permanent.

On the other side of the debate, two pharmacists from downstate Edwardsville, Ill., filed suit against the governor and his emergency rule last week, saying it infringed on their right to weigh their own "conscientious convictions" while carrying out their work. A third pharmacist filed a similar suit on Friday.

But pharmacists and many of their advocates argue that, in reality, only a small number of pharmacists have found themselves in standoffs with customers over the issue.

"There's so much of a spotlight on those very few cases," said Susan C. Winckler, of the American Pharmacists Association, a Washington-based group that represents about 52,000 pharmacists. "This has left some people seeming to say that a pharmacist is nothing more than a garbage man, and that's not what the average pharmacist wants to hear."

The association supports a position that pharmacists should be allowed to "step away" from dispensing items they oppose, while still finding a way to ensure that the customer has access to the items some other way—another pharmacist or another store, for example.

While a few doctors and pharmacists have for years declined to prescribe or sell birth control pills for religious reasons, the objections of some to the morning-after pill are more vehement because they consider it to be more akin to abortion.

The reason the morning-after pill has touched off such debate hinges on the way each side sees the drug, which is also known as Plan B or the emergency contraceptive pill.

Abortion rights advocates and most physicians say the pill, unlike the French drug RU-486, is not an abortion drug because it does not destroy an embryo. Instead, the pill prevents ovulation or fertilization, or blocks a fertilized egg from becoming implanted in the uterus.

Proponents feel it is critical for many pharmacists to offer the morning-after pill because women have only a small window of time after sex in which to obtain and use it. The pill is effective up to three to five days after intercourse, and it is most effective when taken immediately.

"This is one of the safest medicines we have available, and it can prevent unplanned pregnancies."—Dr. Karen Lifford, Planned Parenthood League of Mass.

Advocates also argue that the pill will lead to fewer abortions.

"This is one of the safest medicines we have available, and it can prevent unplanned pregnancies," said Dr. Karen Lifford, the medical director of the Planned Parenthood League of Massachusetts, who testified at a public hearing last week on a bill being considered by the Massachusetts legislature. "We're trying to reduce the number of pregnancies and abortions, and people of different religious views can agree that this is a good thing to do."

But many abortion opponents believe the morning-after pill ends a human life and is therefore tantamount to abortion.

"Emergency contraceptive pills can be abortifacient if they are taken after ovulation has occurred," Dr. Gertrude Murphy, a retired physician who worked at a Catholic hospital in Boston and is currently on the board of Massachusetts Citizens for Life, testified at the hearing. "An abortifacient is defined here as any medication or device that causes the death of the developing human after fertilization."

Around the country, in at least 12 states, including Indiana, Texas, and Tennessee, so-called conscience clause bills have been introduced, which would allow pharmacists to refuse to dispense contraceptives if they have moral or religious objections. Four states already have such laws applying specifically to pharmacists: Arkansas, South Dakota, Mississippi, and Georgia.

Proposals in three states—California, Missouri, and New Jersey—would have the opposite effect, compelling pharmacies to fill any legal prescription.

In California, West Virginia, and a few other states, there is a legislative tug of war, with both types of bills pending in the legislature. In Arizona last week, Gov. Janet Napolitano, a Democrat, vetoed a bill that would have allowed pharmacists to refuse to dispense such drugs.

On the federal level, bills requiring all legal prescriptions to be filled have been introduced in recent days by Senator Barbara Boxer of California and Senator Frank R. Lautenberg of New Jersey. A House version of the Lautenberg bill has been sponsored by Representatives Carolyn B. Maloney of New York and Debbie Wasserman-Schultz of Florida, both Democrats, and Representative Christopher Shays, Republican of Connecticut, among others. The bills are not expected to get very far.

Senator John Kerry, Democrat of Massachusetts, and Senator Rick Santorum, Republican of Pennsylvania, have introduced the Workplace Religious Freedom Act, which would allow a pharmacist to refuse to dispense certain drugs as long as another pharmacist on duty would.

In other states, the battle has less to do with pharmacists' moral beliefs than with efforts by advocates to make emergency contraception more widely available.

Six states—California, Alaska, Hawaii, Maine, New Mexico and Washington—already have laws that skirt the lack of FDA. approval of over-the-counter sales of Plan B. These laws, called collaborative practice measures, allow pharmacists to dispense the morning-after pill if they have received training or certification from the state and are working in collaboration with a physician. Eight other states, including New York and Massachusetts, are considering similar laws.

The Massachusetts law would also require hospitals to inform rape victims about the pill, something Catholic hospitals, in particular, object to. Colorado's governor, Bill Owens, a Republican and a Catholic, vetoed such a bill this month, saying in his explanation, "it is one of the central tenets of a free society that individuals and institutions should not be coerced by government to engage in activities that violate their moral or religious beliefs."

As the debate grows among lawmakers, a quieter debate is taking place behind the counters of many drugstores.

"As far as being a health care professional, I don't think I should be injecting my moral values on other people," Rod Adams, a pharmacist at the Colorado Pharmacy in Denver, said in an interview last week. "Obviously a morning-after pill is a personal choice that someone has to make. They've already made that choice when they come in here, and I don't think—I'm not a counselor—I don't really think that's my job."

But Patty Levin, a pharmacist for 22 years who works at Wender & Roberts in the north Atlanta suburb of Sandy Springs, said that she had never been asked to fill a prescription for the morning-after pill.

"I would be opposed to dispensing that particular product," she said. "It's basically an early abortion, is basically what it is. I would just hand it to the other pharmacist here," she said, adding, "If I'm not filling it, it doesn't involve me."

Appendix

Gender Gap Index

The following charts are taken from *Women's Empowerment: Measuring the Global Gender Gap*, published in 2005 by the World Economic Forum. The study measures the extent to which women in 58 countries have achieved equality with men by rating their economic participation, economic opportunity, political empowerment, educational attainment, and health and well-being.

The Gender Gap Rankings

Country	Overall rank	Overall score*	Economic participation	Economic opportunity	Political empowerment	Educational attainment	Health and well-being
Sweden	1	5.53	5	12	8	1	1
Norway	2	5.39	13	2	3	6	9
Iceland	3	5.32	17	7	2	7	6
Denmark	4	5.27	6	1	20	5	2
Finland	5	5.19	12	17	4	10	4
New Zealand	6	4.89	16	47	1	11	26
Canada	7	4.87	7	27	11	12	14
United Kingdom	8	4.75	21	41	5	4	28
Germany	9	4.61	20	28	6	34	10
Australia	10	4.61	15	25	22	17	18
Latvia	11	4.60	4	6	10	24	48
Lithuania	12	4.58	10	11	13	19	44
France	13	4.49	31	9	14	31	17
Netherlands	14	4.48	32	16	7	42	8
Estonia	15	4.47	8	5	30	18	46
Ireland	16	4.40	37	51	12	9	12
United States	17	4.40	19	46	19	8	42
Costa Rica	18	4.36	49	30	9	14	30
Poland	19	4.36	25	19	18	20	38
Belgium	20	4.30	35	37	25	15	16
Slovak Republic	21	4.28	14	33	29	23	35
Slovenia	22	4.25	26	15	39	22	19
Portugal	23	4.21	27	18	31	36	20
Hungary	24	4.19	30	3	28	39	40
Czech Republic	25	4.19	24	4	43	25	23
Luxembourg	26	4.15	48	8	33	21	25
Spain	27	4.13	45	34	27	35	5
Austria	28	4.13	42	22	21	38	13
Bulgaria	29	4.06	11	14	23	50	55
Colombia	30	4.06	41	38	15	13	52

The Gender Gap Rankings (cont'd)

Country	Overall rank	Overall score*	Economic participation	Economic opportunity	Political empowerment	Educational attainment	Health and well-being
Russian Federation	31	4.03	3	10	47	29	57
Uruguay	32	4.01	36	26	36	2	56
China	33	4.01	9	23	40	46	36
Switzerland	34	3.97	43	42	17	49	7
Argentina	35	3.97	55	29	26	3	54
South Africa	36	3.95	39	56	16	30	21
Israel	37	3.94	28	40	32	28	39
Japan	38	3.75	33	52	54	26	3
Bangladesh	39	3.74	18	53	42	37	37
Malaysia	40	3.70	40	36	51	32	15
Romania	41	3.70	23	31	35	51	47
Zimbabwe	42	3.66	2	57	34	52	41
Malta	43	3.65	56	43	45	16	24
Thailand	44	3.61	1	39	49	54	32
Italy	45	3.50	51	49	48	41	11
Indonesia	46	3.50	29	24	46	53	29
Peru	47	3.47	50	44	38	47	31
Chile	48	3.46	52	20	44	40	45
Venezuela	49	3.42	38	13	52	33	58
Greece	50	3.41	44	48	50	45	22
Brazil	51	3.29	46	21	57	27	53
Mexico	52	3.28	47	45	41	44	51
India	53	3.27	54	35	24	57	34
Korea	54	3.18	34	55	56	48	27
Jordan	55	2.96	58	32	58	43	43
Pakistan	56	2.90	53	54	37	58	33
Turkey	57	2.67	22	58	53	55	50
Egypt	58	2.38	57	50	55	56	49

* All scores are reported on a scale of 1 to 7, with 7 representing maximum gender equality.

The graphs below reflect the performance of particular geographic regions in the World Economic Forum's Gender Gap Rankings.

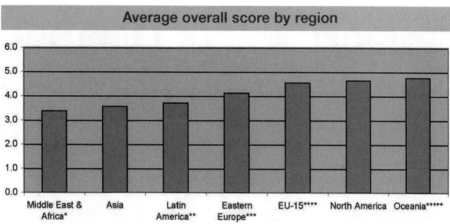

*includes Israel, **includes Mexico, ***includes Russia and Turkey, ****includes the 15 members of the EU before May 2004 and Iceland, ***** includes Australia and New Zealand

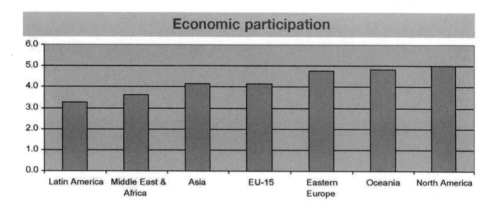

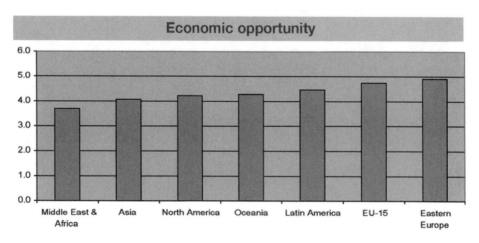

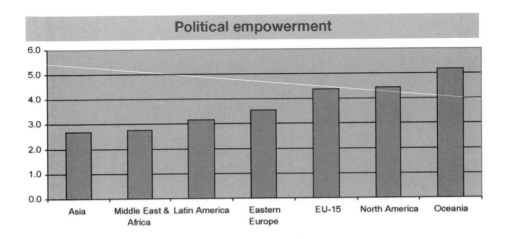

Political empowerment

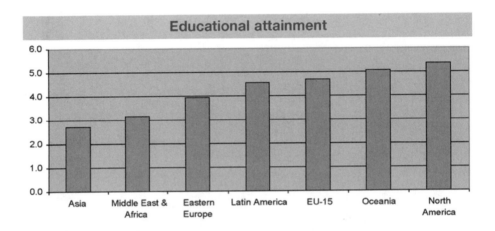

Educational attainment

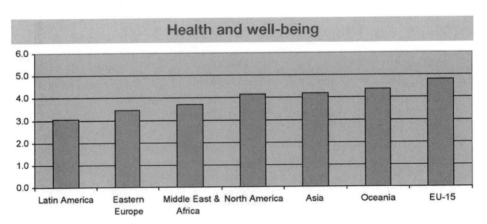

Health and well-being

Shirin Ebadi—Nobel Lecture

DECEMBER 10, 2003

Shirin Ebadi was awarded the Nobel Peace Prize in 2003 for her work promoting democracy and human rights in her native Iran. In 1975 Ebadi became the first woman to serve as a judge in Iran, but, along with all of the subsequently appointed female judges, she was dismissed from her post after the Islamic Revolution in 1979. Since her dismissal, she has fought for social justice as an attorney and has authored several books on human rights and the law.

In the name of the God of Creation and Wisdom
Your Majesty, Your Royal Highnesses, Honourable Members of the Norwegian Nobel Committee, Excellencies, Ladies, and Gentlemen,

I feel extremely honoured that today my voice is reaching the people of the world from this distinguished venue. This great honour has been bestowed upon me by the Norwegian Nobel Committee. I salute the spirit of Alfred Nobel and hail all true followers of his path.

This year, the Nobel Peace Prize has been awarded to a woman from Iran, a Muslim country in the Middle East.

Undoubtedly, my selection will be an inspiration to the masses of women who are striving to realize their rights, not only in Iran but throughout the region—rights taken away from them through the passage of history. This selection will make women in Iran, and much further afield, believe in themselves. Women constitute half of the population of every country. To disregard women and bar them from active participation in political, social, economic, and cultural life would in fact be tantamount to depriving the entire population of every society of half its capability. The patriarchal culture and the discrimination against women, particularly in the Islamic countries, cannot continue for ever.

Honourable members of the Norwegian Nobel Committee!

As you are aware, the honour and blessing of this prize will have a positive and far-reaching impact on the humanitarian and genuine endeavours of the people of Iran and the region. The magnitude of this blessing will embrace every freedom-loving and peace-seeking individual, whether they are women or men.

I thank the Norwegian Nobel Committee for this honour that has been bestowed upon me and for the blessing of this honour for the peace-loving people of my country.

Today coincides with the 55th anniversary of the adoption of the Universal Declaration of Human Rights, a declaration which begins with the recognition of the inherent dignity and the equal and inalienable rights of all members of the human family, as the guarantor of freedom, justice, and peace. And it promises a world in which human beings shall enjoy freedom of expression and opinion, and be safeguarded and protected against fear and poverty.

Unfortunately, however, this year's report by the United Nations Development Programme (UNDP), as in the previous years, spells out the rise of a disaster which distances mankind from the idealistic world of the authors of the Universal Declaration of Human Rights. In 2002, almost 1.2 billion human beings lived in glaring poverty, earning less than one dollar a day. Over 50 countries were caught up in war or natural disasters. AIDS has so far claimed the lives of 22 million individuals, and turned 13 million children into orphans.

At the same time, in the past two years, some states have violated the universal principles and laws of human rights by using the events of 11 September and the war on international terrorism as a pretext. The United Nations General Assembly Resolution 57/219, of 18 December 2002, the United Nations Security Council Resolution 1456, of 20 January 2003, and the United Nations Commission on Human Rights Resolution 2003/68, of 25 April 2003, set out and underline that all states must ensure that any measures taken to combat terrorism must comply with all their obligations under international law, in particular international human rights and humanitarian law. However, regulations restricting human rights and basic freedoms, special bodies, and extraordinary courts, which make fair adjudication difficult and at times impossible, have been justified and given legitimacy under the cloak of the war on terrorism.

The concerns of human rights' advocates increase when they observe that international human rights laws are breached not only by their recognized opponents under the pretext of cultural relativity, but that these principles are also violated in Western democracies, in other words countries which were themselves among the initial codifiers of the United Nations Charter and the Universal Declaration of Human Rights. It is in this framework that, for months, hundreds of individuals who were arrested in the course of military conflicts have been imprisoned in Guantanamo, without the benefit of the rights stipulated under the international Geneva conventions, the Universal Declaration of Human Rights, and the [United Nations] International Covenant on Civil and Political Rights.

Moreover, a question which millions of citizens in the international civil society have been asking themselves for the past few years, particularly in recent months, and continue to ask, is this: why is it that some decisions and resolutions of the U.N. Security Council are binding, while some other resolutions of the council have no binding force? Why is it that in the past 35 years, dozens of U.N. resolutions concerning the occupation of the Palestinian territories by the state of Israel have not been implemented promptly, yet, in the past 12 years, the state and people of Iraq, once on the recommendation of the Security Council, and the second time, in spite of U.N. Security Council opposition, were subjected to attack, military assault, economic sanctions, and, ultimately, military occupation?

Ladies and Gentlemen,

Allow me to say a little about my country, region, culture, and faith.

I am an Iranian. A descendent of Cyrus The Great. The very emperor who proclaimed at the pinnacle of power 2500 years ago that ". . . he would not reign over the people if they did not wish it." And [he] promised not to force any person to change his religion and faith and guaranteed freedom for all. The Charter of Cyrus The Great is one of the most important documents that should be studied in the history of human rights.

I am a Muslim. In the Koran the Prophet of Islam has been cited as saying: "Thou shalt believe in thine faith and I in my religion." That same divine book sees the mission of all prophets as that of inviting all human beings to uphold justice. Since the advent of Islam, too, Iran's civilization and culture has become imbued and infused with humanitarianism, respect for the life, belief, and faith of others, propagation of tolerance and compromise, and avoidance of violence, bloodshed, and war. The luminaries of Iranian literature, in particular our Gnostic literature, from Hafiz, Mowlavi [better known in the West as Rumi] and Attar to Saadi, Sanaei, Naser Khosrow, and Nezami, are emissaries of this humanitarian culture. Their message manifests itself in this poem by Saadi:

> The sons of Adam are limbs of one another
> Having been created of one essence.
> When the calamity of time afflicts one limb
> The other limbs cannot remain at rest.

The people of Iran have been battling against consecutive conflicts between tradition and modernity for over 100 years. By resorting to ancient traditions, some have tried and are trying to see the world through the eyes of their predecessors and to deal with the problems and difficulties of the existing world by virtue of the values of the ancients. But, many others, while respecting their historical and cultural past and their religion and faith, seek to go forth in step with world developments and not lag behind the caravan of civilization, development, and progress. The people of Iran, particularly in the recent years, have shown that they deem participation in public affairs to be their right, and that they want to be masters of their own destiny.

This conflict is observed not merely in Iran, but also in many Muslim states. Some Muslims, under the pretext that democracy and human rights are not compatible with Islamic teachings and the traditional structure of Islamic societies, have justified despotic governments, and continue to do so. In fact, it is not so easy to rule over a people who are aware of their rights, using traditional, patriarchal, and paternalistic methods.

Islam is a religion whose first sermon to the Prophet begins with the word "Recite!" The

Koran swears by the pen and what it writes. Such a sermon and message cannot be in conflict with awareness, knowledge, wisdom, freedom of opinion and expression, and cultural pluralism.

The discriminatory plight of women in Islamic states, too, whether in the sphere of civil law or in the realm of social, political, and cultural justice, has its roots in the patriarchal and male-dominated culture prevailing in these societies, not in Islam. This culture does not tolerate freedom and democracy, just as it does not believe in the equal rights of men and women, and the liberation of women from male domination (fathers, husbands, brothers . . .), because it would threaten the historical and traditional position of the rulers and guardians of that culture.

One has to say to those who have mooted the idea of a clash of civilizations, or prescribed war and military intervention for this region, and resorted to social, cultural, economic, and political sluggishness of the South in a bid to justify their actions and opinions, that if you consider international human rights laws, including the nations' right to determine their own destinies, to be universal, and if you believe in the priority and superiority of parliamentary democracy over other political systems, then you cannot think only of your own security and comfort, selfishly and contemptuously. A quest for new means and ideas to enable the countries of the South, too, to enjoy human rights and democracy, while maintaining their political independence and territorial integrity of their respective countries, must be given top priority by the United Nations in respect of future developments and international relations.

The decision by the Nobel Peace Committee to award the 2003 prize to me, as the first Iranian and the first woman from a Muslim country, inspires me and millions of Iranians and nationals of Islamic states with the hope that our efforts, endeavours, and struggles toward the realization of human rights and the establishment of democracy in our respective countries enjoy the support, backing, and solidarity of international civil society. This prize belongs to the people of Iran. It belongs to the people of the Islamic states, and the people of the South for establishing human rights and democracy.

Ladies and Gentlemen,

In the introduction to my speech, I spoke of human rights as a guarantor of freedom, justice, and peace. If human rights fail to be manifested in codified laws or put into effect by states, then, as rendered in the preamble of the Universal Declaration of Human Rights, human beings will be left with no choice other than staging a "rebellion against tyranny and oppression." A human being divested of all dignity, a human being deprived of human rights, a human being gripped by starvation, a human being beaten by famine, war, and illness, a humiliated human being, and a plundered human being is not in any position or state to recover the rights he or she has lost.

If the 21st century wishes to free itself from the cycle of violence, acts of terror and war, and avoid repetition of the experience of the 20th century—that most disaster-ridden century of humankind—there is no other way except by understanding and putting into practice every human right for all mankind, irrespective of race, gender, faith, nationality, or social status.

In anticipation of that day.

With much gratitude

Shirin Ebadi

Wangari Maathai—Nobel Lecture

DECEMBER 10, 2004

The Norwegian Nobel Committee selected Wangari Maathai for the 2004 Nobel Peace Prize because of her contribution to sustainable development, democracy, and peace in her native Kenya and throughout Africa. In 1971 she became the first woman in East and Central Africa to earn a doctorate, after receiving her Ph. D. in anatomy from the University of Nairobi. Maathai went on to found the Green Belt Movement, a broad-based, grassroots organization that encourages women to plant trees in order to conserve resources and improve their quality of life.

Your Majesties, Your Royal Highnesses, Honourable Members of the Norwegian Nobel Committee, Excellencies, Ladies, and Gentlemen,

I stand before you and the world humbled by this recognition and uplifted by the honour of being the 2004 Nobel Peace Laureate.

As the first African woman to receive this prize, I accept it on behalf of the people of Kenya and Africa, and indeed the world. I am especially mindful of women and the girl child. I hope it will encourage them to raise their voices and take more space for leadership. I know the honour also gives a deep sense of pride to our men, both old and young. As a mother, I appreciate the inspiration this brings to the youth and urge them to use it to pursue their dreams.

Although this prize comes to me, it acknowledges the work of countless individuals and groups across the globe. They work quietly and often without recognition to protect the environment, promote democracy, defend human rights, and ensure equality between women and men. By so doing, they plant seeds of peace. I know they, too, are proud today. To all who feel represented by this prize I say use it to advance your mission and meet the high expectations the world will place on us.

This honour is also for my family, friends, partners, and supporters throughout the world. All of them helped shape the vision and sustain our work, which was often accomplished under hostile conditions. I am also grateful to the people of Kenya—who remained stubbornly hopeful that democracy could be realized and their environment managed sustainably. Because of this support, I am here today to accept this great honour.

I am immensely privileged to join my fellow African Peace laureates, Presidents Nelson Mandela and F.W. de Klerk, Archbishop Desmond Tutu, the late Chief Albert Luthuli, the late Anwar el-Sadat, and the U.N. Secretary General, Kofi Annan.

I know that African people everywhere are encouraged by this news. My fellow Africans, as we embrace this recognition, let us use it to intensify our commitment to our people, to reduce conflicts and poverty, and thereby improve their quality of life. Let us embrace democratic governance, protect human rights, and protect our environment. I am confident that we shall rise to the occasion. I have always believed that solutions to most of our problems must come from us.

In this year's prize, the Norwegian Nobel Committee has placed the critical issue of environment and its linkage to democracy and peace before the world. For their visionary action, I am profoundly grateful. Recognizing that sustainable development, democracy, and peace are indivisible is an idea whose time has come. Our work over the past 30 years has always appreciated and engaged these linkages.

My inspiration partly comes from my childhood experiences and observations of Nature in rural Kenya. It has been influenced and nurtured by the formal education I was privileged to receive in Kenya, the United States, and Germany. As I was growing up, I witnessed forests being cleared and replaced by commercial plantations, which destroyed local biodiversity and the capacity of the forests to conserve water.

Excellencies, ladies, and gentlemen,

In 1977, when we started the Green Belt Movement, I was partly responding to needs identified by rural women, namely lack of firewood, clean drinking water, balanced diets, shelter, and income.

Throughout Africa, women are the primary caretakers, holding significant responsibility for tilling the land and feeding their families. As a result, they are often the first to become aware of environmental damage as resources become scarce and incapable of sustaining their families.

The women we worked with recounted that unlike in the past, they were unable to meet their basic needs. This was due to the degradation of their immediate environment as well as the introduction of commercial farming, which replaced the growing of household food crops. But international trade controlled the price of the exports from these small-scale farmers and a reasonable and just income could not be guaranteed. I came to understand that when the environment is destroyed, plundered, or mismanaged, we undermine our quality of life and that of future generations.

Tree planting became a natural choice to address some of the initial basic needs identified by women. Also, tree planting is simple, attainable, and guarantees quick, successful results within a reasonable amount [of] time. This sustains interest and commitment.

So, together, we have planted over 30 million trees that provide fuel, food, shelter, and income to support their children's education and household needs. The activity also creates employment and improves soils and watersheds. Through their involvement, women gain some degree of power over their lives, especially their social and economic position and relevance in the family. This work continues.

Initially, the work was difficult because historically our people have been persuaded to believe that because they are poor, they lack not only capital, but also knowledge and skills to address their challenges. Instead they are conditioned to believe that solutions to their problems must come from "outside." Further, women did not realize that meeting their needs depended on their environment being healthy and well managed. They were also unaware that a degraded environment leads to a scramble for scarce resources and may culminate in poverty and even conflict. They were also unaware of the injustices of international economic arrangements.

In order to assist communities to understand these linkages, we developed a citizen education program, during which people identify their problems, the causes, and possible solutions. They then make connections between their own personal actions and the problems they witness in the environment and in society. They learn that our world is confronted with a litany of woes: corruption, violence against women and children, disruption and breakdown of families, and disintegration of cultures and communities. They also identify the abuse of drugs and chemical substances, especially among young people. There are also devastating diseases that are defying cures or occurring in epidemic proportions. Of particular concern are HIV/AIDS, malaria, and diseases associated with malnutrition.

On the environment front, they are exposed to many human activities that are devastating to the environment and societies. These include widespread destruction of ecosystems, especially through deforestation, climatic instability, and contamination in the soils and waters that all contribute to excruciating poverty.

In the process, the participants discover that they must be part of the solutions. They realize their hidden potential and are empowered to overcome inertia and take action. They come to recognize that they are the primary custodians and beneficiaries of the environment that sustains them.

Entire communities also come to understand that while it is necessary to hold their governments accountable, it is equally important that in their own relationships with each other, they exemplify the leadership values they wish to see in their own leaders, namely justice, integrity, and trust.

Although initially the Green Belt Movement's tree planting activities did not address issues of democracy and peace, it soon became clear that responsible governance of the environment was impossible without democratic space. Therefore, the tree became a symbol for the democratic struggle in Kenya. Citizens were mobilised to challenge widespread abuses of power, corruption, and environmental mismanagement. In Nairobi's Uhuru Park, at Freedom Corner, and in many parts of the country, trees of peace were planted to demand the release of prisoners of conscience and a peaceful transition to democracy.

Through the Green Belt Movement, thousands of ordinary citizens were mobilised and empowered to take action and effect change. They learned to overcome fear and a sense of help-lessness and moved to defend democratic rights.

In time, the tree also became a symbol for peace and conflict resolution, especially during eth-nic conflicts in Kenya when the Green Belt Movement used peace trees to reconcile disputing communities. During the ongoing re-writing of the Kenyan constitution, similar trees of peace were planted in many parts of the country to promote a culture of peace. Using trees as a sym-bol of peace is in keeping with a widespread African tradition. For example, the elders of the Kikuyu carried a staff from the thigi tree that, when placed between two disputing sides, caused them to stop fighting and seek reconciliation. Many communities in Africa have these traditions.

Such practises are part of an extensive cultural heritage, which contributes both to the con-servation of habitats and to cultures of peace. With the destruction of these cultures and the introduction of new values, local biodiversity is no longer valued or protected and as a result, it is quickly degraded and disappears. For this reason, The Green Belt Movement explores the concept of cultural biodiversity, especially with respect to indigenous seeds and medicinal plants.

As we progressively understood the causes of environmental degradation, we saw the need for good governance. Indeed, the state of any country's environment is a reflection of the kind of governance in place, and without good governance there can be no peace. Many countries which have poor governance systems are also likely to have conflicts and poor laws protecting the environment.

In 2002, the courage, resilience, patience, and commitment of members of the Green Belt Movement, other civil society organizations, and the Kenyan public culminated in the peaceful transition to a democratic government and laid the foundation for a more stable society.

Excellencies, friends, ladies, and gentlemen,

It is 30 years since we started this work. Activities that devastate the environment and societ-ies continue unabated. Today we are faced with a challenge that calls for a shift in our thinking, so that humanity stops threatening its life-support system. We are called to assist the Earth to heal her wounds and in the process heal our own—indeed, to embrace the whole creation in all its diversity, beauty, and wonder. This will happen if we see the need to revive our sense of belonging to a larger family of life, with which we have shared our evolutionary process.

In the course of history, there comes a time when humanity is called to shift to a new level of consciousness, to reach a higher moral ground. A time when we have to shed our fear and give hope to each other.

That time is now.

The Norwegian Nobel Committee has challenged the world to broaden the understanding of peace: there can be no peace without equitable development; and there can be no development without sustainable management of the environment in a democratic and peaceful space. This shift is an idea whose time has come.

I call on leaders, especially from Africa, to expand democratic space and build fair and just societies that allow the creativity and energy of their citizens to flourish.

Those of us who have been privileged to receive education, skills, and experiences and even power must be role models for the next generation of leadership. In this regard, I would also like to appeal for the freedom of my fellow laureate Aung San Suu Kyi so that she can continue her work for peace and democracy for the people of Burma and the world at large.

Culture plays a central role in the political, economic, and social life of communities. Indeed, culture may be the missing link in the development of Africa. Culture is dynamic and evolves over time, consciously discarding retrogressive traditions, like female genital mutilation (FGM), and embracing aspects that are good and useful.

Africans, especially, should re-discover positive aspects of their culture. In accepting them, they would give themselves a sense of belonging, identity, and self-confidence.

Ladies and gentlemen,

There is also need to galvanize civil society and grassroots movements to catalyse change. I call upon governments to recognize the role of these social movements in building a critical mass of responsible citizens, who help maintain checks and balances in society. On their part, civil society should embrace not only their rights but also their responsibilities.

Further, industry and global institutions must appreciate that ensuring economic justice, equity, and ecological integrity are of greater value than profits at any cost.

The extreme global inequities and prevailing consumption patterns continue at the expense of the environment and peaceful co-existence. The choice is ours.

I would like to call on young people to commit themselves to activities that contribute toward achieving their long-term dreams. They have the energy and creativity to shape a sustainable future. To the young people I say, you are a gift to your communities and indeed the world. You are our hope and our future.

The holistic approach to development, as exemplified by the Green Belt Movement, could be embraced and replicated in more parts of Africa and beyond. It is for this reason that I have established the Wangari Maathai Foundation to ensure the continuation and expansion of these activities. Although a lot has been achieved, much remains to be done.

Excellencies, ladies, and gentlemen,

As I conclude I reflect on my childhood experience when I would visit a stream next to our home to fetch water for my mother. I would drink water straight from the stream. Playing among the arrowroot leaves I tried in vain to pick up the strands of frogs' eggs, believing they were beads. But every time I put my little fingers under them they would break. Later, I saw thousands of tadpoles: black, energetic, and wriggling through the clear water against the background of the brown earth. This is the world I inherited from my parents.

Today, over 50 years later, the stream has dried up, women walk long distances for water, which is not always clean, and children will never know what they have lost. The challenge is to restore the home of the tadpoles and give back to our children a world of beauty and wonder.

Thank you very much.

Bibliography

Books

Afkhami, Mahnaz. *Faith and Freedom: Women's Human Rights in the Muslim World.* Syracuse, N.Y.: Syracuse Univ. Press, 1996.

Agosin, Marjorie, ed. *Women, Gender, and Human Rights: A Global Perspective.* Piscataway, N.J.: Rutgers University Press, 2001.

Annas, George J., et al., eds. *Health and Human Rights: A Reader.* New York: Routledge, 1999.

Baer, Judith A. *Historical and Multicultural Encyclopedia of Women's Reproductive Rights in the United States.* Westport, Conn.: Greenwood Press, 2002.

Bayes, Jane H., and Nayereh Tohidi, eds. *Globalization, Gender, and Religion: The Politics of Women's Rights in Catholic and Muslim Contexts.* New York: Palgrave, 2001.

Benedek, Wolfgang, Esther M. Kisaakye, and Gerd Oberleitner, eds. *The Human Rights of Women: International Instruments and African Experiences.* London: Zed Books, 2002.

Chaudhuri, Maitrayee. *Feminism in India.* New York: Zed Books, 2005.

Doezema, Jo, and Kempadoo Kamala, eds. *Global Sex Workers: Rights, Resistance, and Redefinition.* New York: Routledge, 1998.

Ehrenreich, Barbara. *Nickel and Dimed: On (Not) Getting By in America.* New York: Owl Books, 2002.

Ehrenreich, Barbara, and Arlie Russell Hochschild, eds. *Global Woman: Nannies, Maids, and Sex Workers in the New Economy.* New York: Owl Books, 2002.

Erb-Leoncavallo, Ann, et al. *Women and HIV/AIDS: Confronting the Crisis.* New York: UNAIDS, UNFPA, and UNIFEM, 2004.

Farr, Kathryn. *Sex Trafficking: The Global Market in Women and Children.* New York: Worth Publishers, 2004.

Gaag, Nikki van der. *The No-nonsense Guide to Women's Rights.* Oxford: New Internationalist, 2004.

Gioseffi, Daniela, ed. *Women on War: An International Collection of Writings from Antiquity to the Present.* New York: Feminist Press at the City University of New York, 2003.

Gruenbaum, Ellen. *The Female Circumcision Controversy: An Anthropological Perspective.* Philadelphia: University of Pennsylvania Press, 2001.

Guzman Bouvard, Marguerite. *Women Reshaping Human Rights: How Extraordinary Activists Are Changing the World.* Wilmington, Del.: SR Books, 1996.

Howland, Courtney W., ed. *Religious Fundamentalisms and the Human Rights of Women.* New York: Palgrave Macmillan, 2001.

Jacobs, Gloria, ed. *Not a Minute More: Ending Violence Against Women*. New York: United Nations Development Fund for Women, 2003.

Kerr, Joanna, and Caroline Sweetman, eds. *Women Reinventing Globalisation*. Oxford: Oxfam, 2004.

Malone, Mary T. *Women & Christianity*. Maryknoll, N.Y.: Orbis Books, 2001–2003.

Manji, Irshad. *The Trouble with Islam Today: A Muslim's Call for Reform in Her Faith*. New York : St. Martin's Press, 2004.

Mernissi, Fatima. *Islam and Democracy: Fear of the Modern World*. Cambridge, Mass.: Perseus Books Group, 2002.

Mernissi, Fatima. *The Veil and the Male Elite: A Feminist Interpretation of Women's Rights in Islam*. Cambridge, Mass.: Perseus Books Group, 1992.

Molyneux, Maxine, and Shahra Razavi, eds. *Gender Justice, Development, and Rights*. New York: Oxford University Press, 2002.

Morgan, Robin. *The Demon Lover: On the Sexuality of Terrorism*. New York: W.W. Norton & Company, 1989.

Nussbaum, Martha C. *Sex & Social Justice*. New York: Oxford University Press, 1999.

Petchesky, Rosalind Pollack. *Global Prescriptions: Gendering Health and Human Rights*. London: Zed Books, 2003.

Peters, Julie, and Andrea Wolper, eds. *Women's Rights, Human Rights: International Feminist Perspectives*. New York: Routledge, 1995.

Rhode, Deborah L., ed. *The Difference "Difference" Makes: Women and Leadership*. Palo Alto, Cal.: Stanford University Press, 2003.

Seager, Joni. *The Penguin Atlas of Women in the World*. New York: Penguin Books, 2003.

Stiglmayer, Alexandra. *Mass Rape: The War Against Women in Bosnia-Herzegovina*. Lincoln: University of Nebraska Press, 1994.

Wadud, Amina. *Qur'an and Woman: Rereading the Sacred Text from a Woman's Perspective*. New York: Oxford University Press, 1999.

Wanyeki, L. Muthoni, ed. *Women and Land in Africa: Culture, Religion, and Realizing Women's Rights*. London: Zed Books, 2003.

Waring, Marilyn. *If Women Counted: A New Feminist Economics*. New York: HarperCollins, 1990.

Weili, Ye, and Ma Xiadong. *Growing Up in the People's Republic: Conversations Between Two Daughters of China's Revolution*. New York: Palgrave, 2005.

Welchman, Lynn, ed. *Women's Rights and Islamic Family Law: Perspectives on Reform*. London: Zed Books, 2004.

Web Sites

This section offers the reader a list of Web sites that can provide more extensive information on issues related to women's rights. These Web sites also include links to other sites that may be of interest. Due to the nature of the Internet, we cannot guarantee the continued existence of a site, but at the time of this book's publication, all of these Internet addresses were operational.

Amnesty International
www.amnesty.org

Amnesty International (AI) is a worldwide campaign dedicated to the promotion of human rights as outlined in the Universal Declaration of Human Rights and other international human rights standards. The organization produces reports on regions of the world as well as topical issues relating to women's rights.

Human Rights Watch—Women's Rights Division
www.humanrightswatch.org/women/

The Women's Rights Division of Human Rights Watch conducts research and produces report to assist human rights activists in their work. Its official Web site provides visitors with reports on current topics—such as violence against women in Pakistan, women's property rights, and trafficking in persons—as well links to international legal standards.

International Committee of the Red Cross
www.icrc.org

An independent, neutral organization, the International Committee of the Red Cross (ICRC) has a permanent mandate under international law to ensure humanitarian protection and assistance for victims of armed conflict. The ICRC provides resources on the effects of war on women and children.

United Nations Development Fund for Women
www.unifem.org

The United Nations Development Fund For Women (UNIFEM) provides financial and technical assistance to projects that foster gender equality. The organization's four strategic goals include reducing women's poverty and exclusion, ending violence against women, reversing the spread of HIV/AIDS among women and girls, and supporting women's leadership in governance and post-conflict reconstruction. The site offers a variety of reports and tools in electronic format.

United Nations, Division for the Advancement of Women
www.un.org/womenwatch/daw/index.html

The Division for the Advancement of Women (DAW) advocates for the participation of women as equal partners with men in all aspects of human endeavor. The organization's site includes the text of the Convention on the Elimination of All Forms of Discrimination Against Women (CEDAW), country reports, and rulings from the Commission on the Status of Women.

U.S. Department of State, Bureau of Democracy, Human Rights, and Labor
www.state.gov/g/drl/hr

The Bureau of Democracy, Human Rights, and Labor strives to provide accurate information regarding human rights abuses and forges relationships with organizations, governments, and multilateral institutions committed to human rights. Every year the bureau produces a collection of highly regarded reports—all of which are available on this site—on the human rights conditions in more than 190 countries.

U.S. Department of State, Office of International Women's Issues
www.state.gov/g/wi/

The Office of International Women's Issues supports programs and policies that help increase women's political participation, economic opportunities, and access to education and health care. The site focuses in particular on the status of women in Iraq and Afghanistan, as well as the Bush administration's attempts to combat trafficking in persons.

Women's Human Rights Net
www.whrnet.org

The WHRnet serves as a portal for women's rights resources on the Web, providing timely news, interviews, and analyses on current issues and policy developments. The site also offers an introduction to women's rights issues worldwide, an overview of U.N./Regional Human Rights Systems, a research tool for accessing relevant online resources, and a comprehensive collection of related links.

Additional Periodical Articles with Abstracts

More information and perspectives on the subject of women's rights can be found in the following articles. Readers who require a more comprehensive selection of articles are advised to consult the *Readers' Guide to Periodical Literature* and other H.W. Wilson publications.

Seventy-Five Years Voicing Women's Rights. Janelle Conaway. *Americas*, v. 55 pp54+ August 2003.

Conaway relates the history of the Inter-American Commission of Women (CIM), which works to advance women's issues ranging from trade and globalization to peace and security. This daunting task began 75 years ago when a group of women, tired of being excluded from the big intergovernmental hemispheric forums, showed up in force at the Sixth International Conference of American States, which had gathered in Havana, Cuba. In its early decades, Conaway writes, the CIM backed and advanced female suffrage. It also became instrumental in developing women's international legal rights. The writer discusses the issues that the group is currently tackling, including the trafficking of woman and children for sexual exploitation in the Americas.

June Zeitlin: Empowering Women, Saving Lives. Starre Vartan. *E: The Environmental Magazine*, v. 15 pp34–35 September/October 2004.

Attorney June Zeitlin is the executive director of the Women's Environment and Development Organization (WEDO), a global advocacy group actively seeking to empower female policymakers everywhere. Founded in 1990, Vartan writes, WEDO has a close involvement with the U.N. on women's issues. In an interview, Zeitlin discusses such topics as the biggest challenges facing women in developing countries, the ways in which globalization and privatization are affecting women's lives, and the next steps for women's empowerment in developing nations.

The Payoff from Women's Rights. Isobel Coleman. *Foreign Affairs*, v. 83 pp80–95 May/June 2004.

For both ethical and economic reasons, Coleman argues, the United States should work to aggressively promote women's rights abroad. Over the last 10 years, significant research has demonstrated that women are vital to economic development, active civil society, and good governance, particularly in developing nations. Given the importance of women to economic development and democratization—both of which are key U.S. foreign policy objectives— Coleman says that Washington should promote their rights by undertaking, consistently and effectively, an increasing number of programs designed to boost women's educational opportunities, their control over resources, and their economic and political participation. By arguing its case in economic terms, writes Coleman, the United States might even overcome the resistance of conservative Muslim nations that have long balked at gender equality.

I Am Going to Burn: Experiences of Iranian Brothel Workers. Roya Karimi-Majd and Kamran D. Rastegar, translator. *Harper's*, v. 308 pp22–25 March 2004.

Rastegar provides excerpts from interviews, conducted by Roya Karimi-Majd for *Zanan*, a women's magazine published in Tehran, with Iranian brothel workers, who explain how they came to work in prostitution.

The Feminization of AIDS. Radhika Sarin. *The Humanist*, v. 63 p6 January/February 2003.

Sarin reports that over 18 million women have HIV/AIDS. In 2001 women accounted for almost 50 percent of adult cases of HIV, and that proportion is still increasing. Women's vulnerability to the disease is due to biological, economic, and social causes. The disease has orphaned over 13 million children under the age of 15, and in areas where women take part in agricultural production, the spread of AIDS has severely endangered food security at the household and community level. The real solution to tackling the disease, asserts Sarin, lies in improving the status of women by means of education, economic empowerment, open communication, and the elimination of violence and sexual coercion.

What Liberation? Kimberley Sevcik. *Mother Jones*, v. 28 pp19–20+ July/August 2003.

Sevcik writes that the arrest of women in Afghanistan for "moral" crimes was supposed to stop after the Taliban were toppled. Shortly before the American bombing of Afghanistan started in October 2001, President Bush proclaimed his outrage over the Taliban's oppression of women. Once the Northern Alliance had forced the Taliban from Kabul, First Lady Laura Bush succeeded her husband in his weekly radio address to comment on the success of the campaign. On the ground, however, the reality is clearly more complicated. UNICEF estimates that 1.2 million girls attended school in Afghanistan in 2002, Savcik reports, and educated women have started returning to work as teachers, doctors, and lawyers, but these improvements are largely restricted to the capital of Kabul, where an international peacekeeping force maintains security. Provincial governors and former warlords, now known as "regional commanders," continue to rule large tracts of Afghanistan, writes Sevcik, issuing restrictive edicts that differ from the Taliban's radical Islamic code only in degree.

Women, Democracy, and Hope: Women Voting in Afghanistan. Kathy Sheridan. *Ms.*, v. 14 pp46–50 Winter 2004.

In many interviews with potential women parliamentary candidates for April 2005 elections in Afghanistan, Sheridan reports, Human Rights Watch discovered that many live in fear for themselves and their families. Health educators, literacy teachers, and women's rights activists regularly see their efforts destroyed by the lack of security for civilians and sanctions for the perpetrators. Afghanistan's supreme court, which should be the last resort for citizens of a democratic country, is presided over by Chief Justice Mawlawi Hadi Fazel Shinwari, the man who demanded gender segregation at a university, managed to have cable TV channels banned for a time, and often charges people with blasphemy, punishable by death under Islamic law. According to Sheridan, a look under Afghanistan's veneer is enough to reveal stories about the brutal oppression of women and the impunity of those who oppress them.

Not Women Anymore . . . : Plight of Congolese Rape Victims. Stephanie Holen. *Ms.*, v. 15 pp56–58 Spring 2005.

Survivors of rape in the Democratic Republic of the Congo face pain, shame, and AIDS, writes Holen. Eight years of war have left the Congo in ruins, and Congolese women have been victims of rape on a scale never witnessed before. The war resulted in the rape of tens of thousands of women, who are now physically ravaged, emotionally terrorized, and financially impoverished. In fact, Holen says, the women are frequently too physically damaged to farm or bear children, and there is such stigma associated with rape in the Congo— where female virginity is prized and the husband of a rape survivor is regarded as having been shamed—that rape survivors are routinely shunned by husbands, parents, and communities.

Population and Gender Equity. Amartya Kumar Sen. *The Nation*, v. 271 pp16–18 July 24–31, 2000.

Sen writes that the most significant and perhaps the most overlooked feature of the population debate is the negative impact of high fertility imposed on women in societies where their voices do not have much power. The promotion of female literacy, female employment opportunities, and family-planning services, in addition to candid and informed public discussion of women's position in society, can improve the voice and decisional role of women in family affairs and also prompt major changes in conceptions of justice and injustice, argues Sen. There is currently a great deal of evidence, based on intercountry comparisons and interregional contrasts within a big nation, that women's empowerment can have an extremely powerful effect in reducing the fertility rate. The writer discusses some of the evidence on the issue from India.

Women Under Siege. Lauren Sandler. *The Nation*, v. 277 pp11–15 December 29, 2003.

Millions of Iraqi women have been living under practical house arrest since the coalition forces took over Baghdad in April, according to Sandler. They find themselves in this situation due to three threats that have come about since the war. First, Saddam Hussein opened his prisons in October 2002, releasing criminals onto Iraq's streets. Second, there was the collapse of the regime and the collapse of law enforcement. Third, tackling a growing human rights crisis for women is a low priority for the Coalition Provisional Authority, leaving women at the mercy of thugs on the streets and the religious parties that have quickly tried to fill the political vacuum. Unless the coalition and the conservative tribal and religious authorities of Iraq are by some means forced to recognize that women are crucial to the future of the nation, Sandler argues, the current situation is not likely to get better.

Letter from Juarez. Mariana Katzarova. *The Nation*, v. 278 p8 March 29, 2004.

The writer discusses the situation in the Mexican border town of Juarez, where protesters are demanding an end to the murders of women and girls. According to the authorities, some 370 young women have been found murdered in Juarez since 1993. Many of the bodies are found sexually abused and dumped in a nearby desert. Seventy more are still missing, but not a single perpetrator has been brought to justice. On February 14, 2004, a protest march, organized by playwright Eve Ensler and the V-Day movement and supported by Amnesty International, brought between 5,000 and 7,000 people from Ciudad Juarez and El Paso to march through the streets of Juarez, Katzarova reports.

Beneath the Hijab: A Woman. Anthony Giddens. *New Perspectives Quarterly*, v. 21 pp9–11 Spring 2004.

Giddens explains that the battle over the wearing of the hijab, or Muslim head scarf, is not confined to France but has a lengthy history and is taking place in many countries. For example, some regions in Germany are proposing similar legislation to that of France, wearing the hijab is banned in Turkey, and Islamic dress has long been regarded in Indonesia as a sign of ignorance and backwardness. The debate about the hijab is intense, emotional, and global but not indicative of a clash of civilizations; rather, it is about the changing position of women, argues Giddens. As a result, the French ban is likely to be counterproductive because the head scarf has so many different meanings and because a universal ban has an echo of the fundamentalism it seeks to oppose.

AIDS Now Compels Africa to Challenge Widows' "Cleansing." Sharon LaFraniere. *The New York Times*, ppA1+ May 11, 2005.

In rural Malawi, Zambia, and Kenya, LaFraniere reports, married men's funerals have ended with a "cleansing ritual" in which their widows are forced to have sex with a husband's relative in order to exorcize his spirit and save their village and the widow from disease or mental illness. Widows have long tolerated the custom, but now the AIDS pandemic ravaging sub-Saharan Africa may end it. Prodded by feminists, political and tribal leaders are now speaking out against cleansing, saying it is one reason for the rapid spread of HIV among women, yet there is resistance to change. The case of Fanny Mbewe, a 23-year-old widow living in the village of Mchinji, Malawi, is discussed.

China Starts to Give Girls Their Due. Jim Yardley. *New York Times Upfront*, v. 137 pp8–9 March 28, 2005.

Yardley writes that the Chinese government is attempting to redress the imbalance created by decades of population controls and a societal preference for males. The State Council has selected a research group to investigate issues including imbalance between the sexes, falling fertility rates, and ways to prepare for China's rapidly aging population, and it may also examine whether China should adopt a nationwide two-child policy. Experts disagree on the influence of China's one-child rule on its lack of girls, with some noting that the problem predates the policy, reports Yardley. Other Asian countries without such policies also have male-dominated populations, but statistics reveal that China's imbalance has increased since the government introduced population controls in the 1970s.

The War Over Fetal Rights. Debra Rosenberg. *Newsweek*, v. 141 pp40–44+ June 9, 2003.

The writer examines how technological advances, changing state laws, and the case involving the murder of Laci Peterson and her unborn son are making the abortion debate an increasingly complex issue.

No Girls, Please: Abortion and Infanticide in Asia. Mary Carmichael. *Newsweek*, v. 143 p50 January 26, 2004.

Carmichael discusses the culture of infanticide and abortion of female fetuses in India, China, and South Korea. Such practices are largely due to the need to have strong boys to work on farms. In wealthy parts of India, clinics routinely use ultrasound and amniocentesis, technologies they might otherwise take advantage of to ensure the health of a fetus, to identify and abort unborn female children. Korean physicians also employ ultrasound to detect gender, and experts believe that 30,000 female fetuses are aborted there every year, Carmichael reports.

A Woman's Right Is in Peril. *The Progressive*, v. 69 pp8–10 April 2005.

The article states that, on the issue of abortion, most Americans are in favor of women having the right to choose, but the opinions of antiabortion zealots dominate debate in Washington and in statehouses throughout the United States. Even as a large number of pro-choice individuals have been concerned about the potential disaster that awaits in the Supreme Court, the Bush administration has pushed antiabortion policies internationally and domestically. Meanwhile, Congress has more fanatical members than in the past, and the battle in the states is fiercely aggressive. Consequently, the article asserts, American women now have much less freedom to have an abortion than they did the day after *Roe v. Wade* was handed down in 1973. For poor women, who are disproportionately of color, that freedom is balanced very precariously.

Her Turn to Pray: Mixed Prayer Service Conducted by Female Islamic Scholar A. Wadud at Cathedral of St. John the Divine. Jeff Chu and Nadia Mustafa. *Time*, v. 165 p49 March 28, 2005.

Chu and Mustafa report on a historic service at the Cathedral Church of St. John the Divine in New York that is seen as indicative of a new drive by Muslim women to reclaim their rights in the mosque. Although many Muslim women throughout the world have embraced the strict gender divisions in traditional Islam, a movement in the United States is endeavoring to meld Muslim teachings with Western ideas of gender equality. On the grounds of the cathedral, the writers report, Amina Wadud recently became the first woman since Islam's earliest days to preside over a publicly held mixed-gender prayer service, according to the organizers who invited her. In spite of protests and angry opposition to the event, organizer Asra Nomani is planning further services.

Taking Gender into Account. Malgorzata Tarasiewicz. *UN Chronicle*, v. 40 p37 December 2003/February 2004.

Tarasiewicz claims that the new information and communication technologies (ICTs) display the same inequality that has existed for decades between women and men. Aside from the difficulty of access to hardware and software, women are rarely in decision-making positions in technology, and due to gender stereotypes, men dominate in management positions. Women should decide for themselves how to use technology for their empowerment, should secure equal access to new employment opportunities, and should have more decision-making roles in information technology, argues Tarasiewicz. The use of ICT as a good tool in disseminating information and advocating gender equality should also be promoted. The World Summit on the Information Society (WSIS) provides a unique means to attract the attention of national governments, international institutions, and the world community to these issues.

Making Mothers Count: The Fiscal Value of Nurturing. Kristin Maschka. *USA Today Magazine*, v. 132 pp26–27 November 2003.

If society is to move forward, Maschka argues, greater value must be placed on women's work within the home. Raising children correctly is an investment in America's collective future, because the country's society and economy depend on developing the workers and citizens of tomorrow. Maschka writes that mothers will attain social and economic equality when productive, contributing "work" is redefined to include unpaid domestic work; public policies and workplaces are reorganized to mirror this new definition; and cultural attitudes regarding the value of caregiving work change. All of these changes will provide both men and women with more options for caring for their families during their lifetimes, says Maschka.

Women in the Workplace—The Unfinished Revolution. Myra H. Strober. *USA Today Magazine*, v. 132 pp28–29 November 2003.

Strober discusses the revolution in relation to the involvement of women in the workplace, which she says remains incomplete. The shift of women to paid labor has resulted in a widespread transformation of the traditional rules and practices of daily life, not just at workplaces but also in families. Nonetheless, if women's jobs call for 30, 40, or more hours a week, Strober says, they are unable to spend these same hours caring for their families. Society has not concentrated on the need to offer alternative types of care, especially for children and the elderly, during the time that caregivers are employed. In order to complete the revolution, new institutions and new arrangements are required, writes Strober. In fact, there must be an active partnership on this issue among employees, employers, and government.

Make Way for the Women. Kevin Whitelaw. *U.S. News & World Report*, v. 138 pp29–31 February 21, 2005.

Whitelaw writes that the level of power handed to women will reveal much about the future of Iraq. In the recent elections, the Shiite coalition known as List 169 appears to have captured approximately half of the seats in the new assembly. Many Iraqis are now concerned that the Shiites, who were oppressed under Saddam Hussein, will attempt to establish a state closer to their own religious vision, with the possible implementation of *sharia*, or Islamic religious law. Although at least one-quarter, and as much as one-third, of the new assembly will be made up of women, says Whitelaw, there are concerns that many of the new female lawmakers will carry little influence.

The Woman Question. Haleh Esfandiari. *The Wilson Quarterly*, v. 28 pp56–63 Spring 2004.

In campaigning for equal rights, claims Esfandiari, women in the Middle East are expanding society's democratic space. Courageous individuals, such as

Iranian activist and Nobel Peace Prize winner Shirin Ebadi, have made women key players in the battle for a more liberal democratic order, and the position of women now serves as a critical barometer of progress. Nonetheless, the writer says, even as a degree of liberalization has occurred in some nations, there has been movement in the opposite direction in others, with key differences in women's status found between countries practicing the Sunni and Shiite forms of Islam. Moreover, equal legal status for women is almost unachievable as long as family law remains based on the Islamic *sharia* and rules derived from a particular interpretation of Islam prevail, argues Esfandiari.

Index